Nostradamus

AND THE NEW MILLENNIUM

A NEW GUIDE TO THE
GREAT SEER'S PROPHECIES

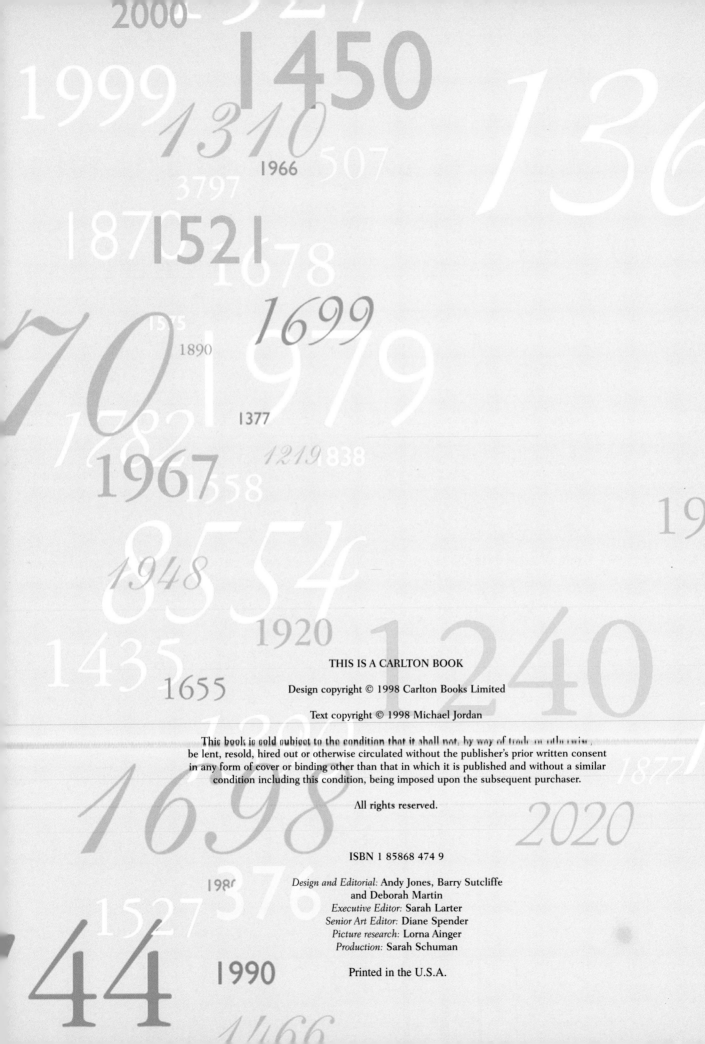

THIS IS A CARLTON BOOK

Design copyright © 1998 Carlton Books Limited

Text copyright © 1998 Michael Jordan

ISBN 1 85868 474 9

Design and Editorial: Andy Jones, Barry Sutcliffe
and Deborah Martin
Executive Editor: Sarah Larter
Senior Art Editor: Diane Spender
Picture research: Lorna Ainger
Production: Sarah Schuman

Printed in the U.S.A.

NOSTRADAMUS

AND THE NEW MILLENNIUM

A NEW GUIDE TO THE GREAT SEER'S PROPHECIES

Michael Jordan

CARLTON

CONTENTS

DURING MUCH OF HUMAN HISTORY *we have been fascinated by the possibility that, amongst some exceptionally gifted individuals, the future may be revealed through prophecy and as we come towards the year 2000 this interest has intensified. Yet such people are also invariably surrounded by controversy and those who claim the power of the seer are regarded as either visionaries or lunatics according to our differing points of view. One such individual who surely ranks amongst the most celebrated of the world's prophets, or madmen, is the obscure sixteenth-century doctor whom the world has come to know as Nostradamus.*

the KEY *to* TIME

nostradamus stands amongst a venerated line of prophets reaching back into biblical times. Most of these extraordinary individuals, including Nostradamus himself, arrived at their prognostications about the future through astrology – the study of the effects on humankind of conjunctions between heavenly bodies. In the succinct words of the celebrated medieval philosopher and physician, Paracelsus, 'all influences that come from the Sun, the planets and the stars, act invisibly on man, and if these are evil, they will produce evil effects'.

If indeed Nostradamus was a visionary then he may, in more senses than one, have been possessed by unusual insight. Apart from the fact that some of his predictions appear to have come true, he set the seal on a futuristic feat of literary endurance which has rarely been equalled before or after his lifetime. It is an astonishing statistic that never once, in the four hundred years or more since the first batch was published by Mace Bonhomme in Lyon in 1555, have the volumes of Nostradamus' prophecies been out of print. Few authors, other than the compilers of the biblical texts, can claim a comparable measure of public accolade sustained over such a long period of time.

What is it about Nostradamus that has stimulated our imaginations so thoroughly and for so long? His predictions are unusual in that a large number of them are of a gloomy or violent nature. They suggest terrible things to come and this has no doubt attracted a level of morbid and vicarious curiosity. For instance,

> *There are new tyrants in Naples, Sicily, Palermo and Syracuse,*
> *thunder and lightning in the skies.*
> *An army from London, Gent, Brussels and Susa;*
> *a great massacre, then triumph and festivities.*

or,

> *A great army will cross over the Alps.*
> *A short time before a wretched monster will be born.*
> *In a strange way suddenly the great Tuscan*
> *will return to his native land.*

PORTRAIT
DE MICHEL NOSTRADAMUS,
Astronome célèbre.

Michel Nostradamus naquit à Saint-Remy, petite ville de Provence, le 14 décembre 1503, à l'heure de midi ; il était fils de Jacques Nostradamus, notaire royal de cette ville, et de damoiselle Renée de Saint-Remy ; il était petit-fils, tant paternel que maternel, de médecins et mathématiciens célèbres ; il fut reçu docteur en l'université de Montpellier, dont il exerça la charge de professeur. Ce grand homme a vécu sous les règnes de Louis XII, François Ier, Henri II et Charles IX, dont il fut médecin ; il retourna à Salon, autre ville de Provence, et y mourut en bon chrétien, après avoir été tourmenté par la goutte qui, dégénérée en hydropisie, le suffoqua au bout de huit jours, ayant prédit l'heure et le jour de sa mort, qui arriva entre trois et quatre heures du matin, le 2 juillet 1566.

Propriété de l'éditeur. (Dé; o:d.)   Fabrique de PELLERIN, Imprimeur-Libraire, à EPINAL.

A NINETEENTH-CENTURY PORTRAIT OF MICHEL DE NOTREDAME, WHOSE ENIGMATIC PROPHECIES HAVE
INTRIGUED THE WORLD FOR MORE THAN FOUR HUNDRED YEARS.

THE INFLUENTIAL SWISS PHYSICAN, ALCHEMIST AND PHILOSOPHER PHILIPPUS PARACELSUS (1493–1541).

It is easy to take many of his enigmatic verses and use one's imagination to play with the various portents they contain, regardless of the period of history in which one lives. But the sheer puzzle of the legacy is also part of the endless fascination which brushes aside the years. Prophecy was highly popular in the sixteenth century, but whilst many of Nostradamus' contemporaries who foresaw future events, published them in such a way that their meaning was fairly obvious, his remained largely obscure with a tantalizing minimum of clues.

Nostradamus was canny enough, in the elusiveness and resistance to interpretation which he crafted into the four-line predictions or *quatrains*, the *sixains* and the separate *présages* or portents, to make them seem timeless.

He left us with an enduring enigma and the intervening centuries since his death have witnessed not only uninterrupted publication of his work but a constant outpouring of attempts to analyse and interpret. About what, and concerning whom, were the predictions made? When will the events so vaguely described, and in such an alleged muddle of chronology, take place? We long to know but the interpretation tantalizes and resists us!

In the popular belief Nostradamus predicted our fate at the turn of the twenty-first century and went so far as to concentrate his gift of foresight on the precise decades in which we live, providing us with dreadful warnings of massive and violent destruction – the scenario of 'apocalypse now'. This is popular guesswork but, perversely, without any substantive basis beyond the febrile imaginations of some modern authors. This is not to say that Nostradamus failed to provide predictions about our present-day world, only that he did not concentrate his prognostications upon us in the manner that some have claimed.

Before we can begin to elucidate what Nostradamus had in store for us living at the close of the twentieth century, however, it is essential to understand Nostradamus the man, his life and his times some 450 years ago. Therein lies the key to his prophecies and without this understanding and insight it will never be possible to climb the ladder of years between his world and ours.

The Appeal of the Mystery

Nostradamus is said to have received the prophecies in detailed visions and signs. Yet not only has he couched many of them in the most veiled terms but, with a few notable exceptions, he has provided none with a specific calendar date. Comparatively few can be aligned with any degree of certainty to events which took place either in Nostradamus' own time or in future eras which have now come and gone and it is a reflection that, out of a little over 960 quatrains, the meanings of no more than 50 have met with anything approaching common agreement amongst analysts. A little less than half the total (about 420 according to some recent estimates) are loosely agreed to have come to fruition but the 'fruits' have, by and large, received widely varying interpretations.

Frequently one finds that quatrains have been ascribed to different events, countries and even to conflicting centuries (in the chronological sense).

The absence of clear meaning is not, however, the main obstacle to decipherment. It is, above all, the elusive chronology which has presented the conundrum because nobody has managed, convincingly, to unravel the secret of the dating. Without the vital code with which to align the prophecies with places and events their interpretation is destined to remain even less realistic than their enigmatic phrasing permits.

The paucity of dating, coupled with the obscurity of the lines and the considerable time-span which they appear to cover, provides the perennial fascination of the prophecies. Yet, by the same token, it is far too easy to play inventive games with Nostradamus' material since it is possible, figuratively, to cut the cloth of his quatrains in more or less any style according to the predictive coat one has in mind. Instances in which selective manipulation of the quatrains has taken place are not difficult to find. **CII, Q3** predicts that:

Pour la chaleur solaire sus la mer
De Negrepont les poissons demy cuits,
Les habitants les viendront entamer,
Quand Rhod et Gennes leur faudra le biscuit.

This small but intriguing insight into an unusual event destined to occur in the Black Sea region has been distorted by more than one author on the grounds that Nostradamus has used a grammatical device for contraction known as the ablative absolute, whereby prepositions and other small words are eliminated. The first line is translated, in popular vogue, to read: *because of a heat like the sun's* as if the preposition has been excluded from the line. The sense created instantly becomes fodder for the imagination because it may be seized upon as indication of a devastating atomic explosion. Unfortunately, the given translation is not an accurate reflection of the French. The line reads more correctly and simply: *because of the heat of the sun*. From the speculative starting point of a nuclear holocaust, the popular interpretation expands to far-fetched extremes suggesting that, despite an explosion of sufficient magnitude to cook the fish in the sea, the people living in the neighbourhood will be unaffected to the extent that they will not only be able to collect up all the steamed *fruits de mer* but sell them to their neighbours in Greece and Italy! This example is not untypical of the urge to dramatize, however ludicrous the interpretation which results.

A similar example of overly liberal interpretation can be found amongst authors focusing on one of the most significant *quatrains* **CX, Q72**. This includes a key word 'Angoulmois' with reference to a great leader whose influence will be felt in 1999. At least one explanation establishes 'Angoulmois' as an anagram (exactly how the anagram is achieved is unclear) of 'Mongolois' and claims

the *quatrain* to be a signal of some imminent invasion of Europe by Mongol hordes from the Orient.

In one sense this type of inventive explanation possesses similarity to a clairvoyant's page from a tabloid newspaper although, unlike the sugar-coated words of the personal horoscope, it is clearly designed to meet the tried and tested journalistic maxim that 'the only good news is bad news'. Even when Nostradamus has not provided dark omens, the modern translator seems determined to create them!

One should also not fall into the trap proclaimed by some 'elitist' authors which promotes the belief that a highly specialized knowledge of etymology is necessary, in

DUBOIS' DEPICTION OF THE FALL OF THE BASTILLE: THE FRENCH REVOLUTION HAS POPULARLY BEEN SEEN AS THE SUBJECT OF MANY OF THE PROPHECIES, YET WITH LITTLE REAL FOUNDATION.

certain instances, in order to uncover the meaning of the text. In his book *Countdown to Apocalypse*, Jean-Charles de Fontbrune offers an example of an alleged difficulty to be found in **CIX, Q34**. The line: *Par cinq cens un trahyr sera titre* is alleged to be incomprehensible without sophisticated linguistic understanding. De Fontbrune, in common with other commentators, makes the laboured point that he is a 'professional translator'. Yet a pocket Anglo-French dictionary will reveal the sense of this line to anyone with a reasonable degree of common sense. The old French noun *trahyr* is easily reached through the modern verb *trahir*, 'to betray', whilst *titrer* is given to have an assortment of meanings including 'to cause'. In other words, 'a betrayal will be caused (orchestrated) by five hundred people'. Not a very difficult translation to achieve!

Crank, Heretic or Genius?

If one is to make a more intelligent, and less sensationalized appraisal of Nostradamus, a number of important questions have to be addressed at the outset. One of them must be to ask whether Nostradamus was a lunatic, or a sane and intelligent man who possessed a remarkable and extra-sensory gift enabling him to probe and record humankind's fate. A second, fundamental query must rest with the purpose of the predictions. What led Nostradamus to write down his prophetic visions in such an enigmatic style? Did he carefully tailor them only to captivate and tantalize endless future generations of his readers in some cruel joke that never reaches a conclusion, conundrums for the sake of conundrums, or is their enigmatic nature a response by Nostradamus to the fraught political and religious climate in which he lived and with which he elected to deal in the most prudent manner open to him? If the latter option is the more accurate, in what manner did Nostradamus provide the code to their understanding?

Madman or inspired visionary? The psychic power to predict what will happen tomorrow and the day after will always remain a highly controversial and sensitive subject, interpretation of future events through the stars only marginally less contentious. If the future course of history is ascertainable, that knowledge presents a profound implication for mankind. The import of such a revelation must be that the human spirit is not free to pursue its own independent will but is governed from cradle to grave by some higher power which directs the course of cosmic events in minute and predetermined detail. Hence, there will always be those who maintain that Nostradamus was an unbalanced eccentric, because to accept anything less would be to reject the belief in our collective ability to fashion a better world for future generations of humanity. Even Paracelsus, regarded as a dangerous radical in his day, was careful to qualify his belief in prophecy. When commenting on astrology he noted: 'the stars are free for themselves and we are free for ourselves'.

The pseudo-science of predicting the future course of events by reference to the stars was a very ancient and respected activity which had begun in ancient Egypt. The Pharaoh Ramesses II, who lived in the thirteenth century BCE, was responsible for fixing the cardinal astrological signs, including Aries, Cancer, Capricorn and Libra. In the second century CE one of his Egyptian successors in astrology, Claudius Ptolomaeus or Ptolemy, wrote the first generally accepted textbook on the subject, the

PTOLEMY USING A QUADRANT TO MEASURE THE ALTITUDE OF THE MOON: AN ILLUSTRATION FROM *MARGARITA PHILOSOPHICA*, PUBLISHED IN 1508.

SCENO
SYSTEMATIS
PTOLE

GRAPHIA
MVNDANI
MAICI.

Tetrabiblos. Ptolemy catalogued more than 1000 stars and, whilst believing that the world of mankind was at the centre of a universe encircled by heavenly bodies, he exercised tremendous influence over later researchers in medieval Europe.

The Catholic Church in the sixteenth century recognized the significance and value of prognostication but with considerable ambivalence. Prophecy was accepted with the proviso that it was not conducted in an anarchic or untutored fashion. In fact the Church was hardly in a position to object to the science of prediction through astrology since it already used astrologers to assist its own needs. In the fifteenth century Pope Sixtus IV had employed a respected German astronomer, Johann Muller, who went under the name Regiomontanus, as papal astrologer ostensibly to assist with the reformation of the calendar but also, it is thought, to advise the papacy on the astrological implications of its war with Florence.

In general terms the Church could not exclude the possibility of messages from God about the future, and vigils at the shrines of saints in order to receive prophetic visions were a common occurrence, perhaps too common. A commentator writing in the mid seventeenth century remarked that 'only the qualified could teach but anyone might be inspired to prophecy'. He was hinting at the establishment view that anything which was accepted as being divinely inspired should generally have come from the upper classes and clerical orders. Many of the prophets who peddled their wares in medieval Europe, however, were at best tradesmen or artisans and, at worst, illiterate. A hundred years after Nostradamus, Oliver Cromwell observed wryly: 'If credence should be given to every such lewd person as would affirm himself to have revelations from God, what readier way were there to subvert all commonwealths and good order in the world?'

Great importance was, therefore, attached to visions, astral predictions, dreams and their interpretation, and other forms of divination, but authorities adopted a selective evaluation according to the source of inspiration.

THIS PAGE FROM A CELESTIAL ATLAS OF THE 1650s SHOWS HOW PTOLEMY'S PLANETARY SYSTEM FEATURED THE EARTH AS THE CENTRE OF THE UNIVERSE.

A FRONTISPIECE OF 1496 DEPICTS PTOLEMY (LEFT) AND REGIOMONTANUS (RIGHT) SEATED BELOW AN ARMILLARY SPHERE, OR CELESTIAL GLOBE, IN WHICH THE EARTH IS SEEN IN THE CENTRE ENCIRCLED BY THE SIGNS OF THE ZODIAC.

On the subject of premonitory dreams, whilst asserting that most which occurred outside of qualified circles were attributable to physical causes such as indigestion, it was conceded that some were of supernatural nature. These, however, were probably more of diabolical than divine origin, and so lay the danger for the dreamer! From the viewpoint of the common man religious visions were regarded as a mark of saintliness and, at street level, interpretation of dreams was a service regularly offered by wizards and astrologers. Martyrs who foretold their own deaths or those of others were also popularly held to have received divine inspiration and it was generally accepted that persons who went about their business in holy fashion were more likely to enjoy a special gift of prophecy than sinners. The gift of foresight was, in short, a potentially dangerous one which could as easily lead to punishment as to reverence.

Detractors from Nostradamus were quick to emerge almost immediately after first publication of the prophecies. Works such as the anonymously written *Declaration des abus, ignorances, seditions de Michel Nostradamus*, published in Avignon in 1558, possess pejorative titles which speak for themselves. When Nostradamus was published in English he received the scorn of the Anglican Church in the form of Archbishop Parker who cast his *Centuries* aside as a 'fantastical hotch-potch'. By and large history already showed that astrological predictions were politically motivated by malcontents and were too frequently linked with conspiracies and uprisings. During the previous fifteenth century a number of astrologers had been executed for such offences as predicting the life expectancy of a monarch which, for obvious reasons, was considered unwelcome. Later, in 1581, the English parliament made it a statutory offence to offer public predictions on how long Queen Elizabeth would live and who would be her successors. It is believed that subversives such as the perpetrators of the Gunpowder Plot were strongly influenced by

PREDICTIONS ABOUT THE LIFESPAN OF ELIZABETH I WERE FORBIDDEN BY ACT OF PARLIAMENT, SUCH WAS THE CREDENCE GIVEN TO ASTROLOGICAL FORECASTS.

THE PARTICIPANTS IN THE GUNPOWDER PLOT OF 1605, DEPICTED IN THIS 1606 ENGRAVING, WERE BELIEVED TO HAVE BEEN INFLUENCED BY POLITICALLY MOTIVATED PREDICTIONS.

this quality of prognostication and it is not hard to see why those in authority took a poor view.

On the other hand there was soon assembled a sizeable lobby of supporters, those who placed Nostradamus in a more favourable light and who were persuaded that his predictions, some of which reflected affairs of their own time, were valid and justifiable. In the following century there was much interest in the wars between England and France and prognosticators on the topic were eagerly read on both sides of the Channel. They included notably, on the English side, a Mr Truswell, the Recorder of Lincoln, and on the French, Michel de Notredame. In 1673, one Chevalier de Jant published a treatise entitled, with characteristic French flair for brevity: *Predictions tirées des Centuries de Nostradamus qui, vraisemblablement peuvent s'expliquer à la guerre entre France et l'Angleterre contre les provinces unies.* De Jant, and like-minded critics, clearly adopted a more sympathetic and responsive tone.

Today, much as in past times, positive subscribers to the abilities of Nostradamus who believe that he has something credible to offer, tend to divide into two philosophical schools. There are those on the fringes of intelligent analysis who argue his utterances to be the ineffable word of God and who frequently claim divine powers of their own, enabling them to decipher the exact meaning of the puzzles. Frequently such authors assert that they are capable of psychic regression, a device which opens the door to communication between students of Nostradamus and the shade of the great seer himself. A brief glance at many of the more obscure published titles, and at the pages of eccentricity expounding on Nostradamus through the modern facility of the Internet, provides an indication of the level of compulsion and eccentric thinking which brings such commentators into a common fold.

Balancing the scales against the detractors have been those of more sensible disposition who have striven towards a scholarly and reasoned approach. The first of these adherents was probably Jean Aime de Chavigny, a close ally of Nostradamus whose attempt to elucidate on the predictions was published in Lyon in 1594. De Chavigny's path was then trodden by an assortment of researchers, some wise, some not, throughout the subsequent centuries running down towards the modern era. Amongst recent authors one can single out the probing works of

Jean-Charles de Fontbrune, following in the footsteps of his father, Max de Fontbrune, Edgar Leoni, and the writings of Erika Cheetham who has provided arguably the best modern English translations, based on the first published edition of Nostradamus. These authors, and others like them, have invested enormous amounts of research into the nature of the prophecies and have given years of detailed and serious study to the precise wording of the *quatrains* and *présages*. Yet all have fallen into the same trap claiming, without any reasonable justification, that the emphasis in Nostradamus' predictive writing is on the close of the twentieth century and the 'apocalypse now' scenario.

The Nature of the Enigma

Not all versions of Nostradamus' prophetic works are the same. The prophecies have now been published in a great many editions, but some of the earlier imprints are undated and it has been established beyond reasonable doubt that a number of these represent forgeries, published at least a hundred years after the dates claimed in their frontispieces and with texts that have been tampered with. Printed editions of the manuscripts have to be examined with caution because there are issues of possible omission and, frequently, a lack of sound provenance. The original texts were first printed in a partial set in 1555, then as the 'complete' work published by Benoit Rigaud in 1558, but potential pitfalls lie in failing to distinguish the various apocryphal versions that keep faith, to a variable extent, with the original.

Translation from the old French presents an added risk. Not all editors of foreign language editions have paid scrupulous attention to the curious linguistic style in which the work was written. This tongue is accountably different in many respects from modern French, its etymology more closely wedded to classical Greek and Latin, and it is prone to cause a measure of error and confusion when inadequately or subjectively handled. Nostradamus confused the etymologist further in that he frequently wrote in Latin, using typical Latin syntax in word order and arrangement, whilst giving the *impression* that he was writing French.

There has been suggestion amongst some authors that Nostradamus also adopted the practice of some Latin writers involving omission of letters or syllables at the beginning, ending or middle of a word in order to scan the verses and to divert unlettered persons from the real meaning of his prophecies. These authors conveniently fail to admit that the supposed aberrations provide even more freedom to exercise wild interpretation. It is very easy to claim that Nostradamus did not actually mean what he wrote and equally impossible to prove or disprove! By similar token it has been claimed that he regularly applied the ablative absolute thereby omitting such elements as prepositions from his sentences. This argument, once again, is largely speculative but serves to increase the licence of the translator.

There are a number of reasons why the argument that Nostradamus disguised his work etymologically does not hold water. In the first place his schooling provided him with only a basic working knowledge of Latin and Greek, insufficient probably to allow him sophisticated manipulation of words. It is known that he made rough translations of some of the minor Classics and that he had used Latin as a physician but this experience would have fallen far short of the linguistic erudition needed.

Although it is claimed that the use of reduced sentences facilitated the ten-syllable or decasyllabic scan which he favoured for the *quatrains* (as well as confusing his detractors) on closer examination many of the lines in the original are not composed with strict attention to decasyllabic form. They may possess nine or eleven syllables. Perhaps the most significant flaw, however, lies in the claim that Nostradamus deliberately gallicised Greek and Latin to prevent commentators who were not classicists from understanding his prophecies. This argument is a nonsense because if any single body was particularly familiar with the vagaries of classical Greek and Roman, it was the ecclesiastical board of inquiry, the Inquisition, whose attentions Nostradamus wished urgently to avoid.

The 1568 version of his work, which will be relied upon here, includes twelve 'Centuries' of predictions amounting to either 964 or 965 *quatrains* composed more or less in decasyllabic verse, 58 *sixains*, 141 *présages*, an isolated *quatrain* composed in Latin, and two letters, one addressed to Nostradamus' son, César, the other to a French king named Henri.

It becomes immediately apparent from the simple mathematics of this list that the *quatrains* are incomplete. There should, theoretically, be twelve hundred but Century VII, for example, includes only forty-six *quatrains*, whilst Century XII has a mere eleven. Even if one includes the single *quatrain* in Latin, the *sixains* and the *présages* there are, in total, no more than 1165 separate predictions. So, is some of the original material missing, or did Nostradamus fail to complete his intended task? Alas, there is no means of knowing and this does little to ease the confusion.

That his works, authentic and apocryphal, have never been out of print is something which Nostradamus, with all his foresight, may not have anticipated because there is no indication that he was a particularly self-aggrandizing man. But had he contented himself with predicting events that would take place during the next decade or even century, he would no doubt have enjoyed short-term notoriety and then faded from our affections, dismissed as another of the quirky characters with which history's broom cupboards are filled. Instead he tantalized posterity with predictions of future events that arguably spanned not just the period until the Christian year 2000, still comparatively interminable in the mid-sixteenth century, but, like some modern space explorer, reached towards the more misty edges of time.

In this illustration of a German herb garden and workshop of the sixteenth century, people can be seen sniffing and picking herbs, explaining their use and one even pouring a concoction on his hair.

Equally, though, he may have had no conscious intention of leaving us scratching our heads. It is difficult to conceive of the man preparing for his deathbed – by the time that the manuscripts were completed a long-term health battle was being lost as gout turned to dropsy – whilst being content to abandon so many years of labour in a form which would remain unintelligible to all but himself. It must be a reasonable guess, therefore, that he left some form of key or coding which posterity might have the wit and wisdom to detect. Yet in the four intervening centuries down to the present time, no Nostradamus-watcher has been able to meet the challenge by playing an effective game of detection. So where have we gone wrong? Have we been searching so deeply that we have missed something obvious?

The Biographical Background

The quest for answers must surely begin with Nostradamus himself and the social, political and religious constraints under which he lived. Michel de Notredame, his given name, was born the eldest of either seven or eight children on 14th December 1503, according to the Julian calendar of the time. There is, however, a paucity of information about his family background. Beyond the fact that his earliest years were spent in the French city of St Rémy de Provence, that his father's name was either Jaume or Jacques, and his mother was Reynière de St Rémy, we know little. The title 'de Notredame' appears to refer merely to his family's local parish and the popular name Nostradamus was coined in later years. Records indicate that Jaume de Notredame had inherited a successful family business as a grain merchant, that Nostradamus' siblings were all male and that his mother and father were of simple Jewish-French stock. It is established that one of the brothers was named César (not to be confused with Nostradamus' son by his second marriage who inherited the *Centuries*) who became the Procureur du Parliament de Provence. The children were brought up, through political expediency, as Roman Catholics rather than in the Jewish faith of their ancestors since Jews were treated with considerable suspicion in the climate of religious bigotry which characterized much of sixteenth-century French life.

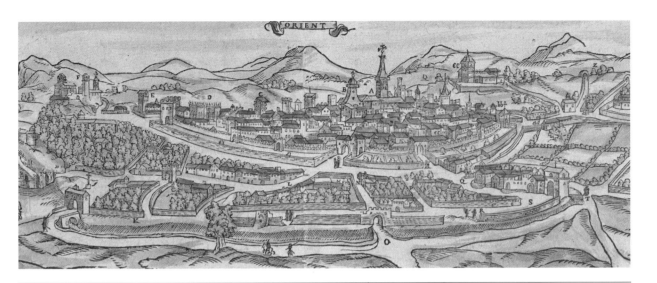

NOSTRADAMUS STUDIED MEDICINE AT THE UNIVERSITY OF MONTPELLIER; THIS VIEW OF THE TOWN IS
CONTEMPORARY WITH HIS LIFETIME.

The intellectual and scholarly influences on Nostradamus, the people in his life who may have played a part in his reasoning before and during the compilation of the prophecies, need to be given serious consideration, however scant our information. His maternal grandfather, Jean, a physician who was well versed in herbalism, the Classics, and, significantly, in astronomy and mathematics, exercised a considerable sway over Nostradamus' childhood and adolescence. He was first schooled by Jean who endowed his pupil with an elementary knowledge of Latin, Greek, Hebrew, mathematics and astronomy, the so-called 'celestial science' of his day which was considered to be inseparable from astrology, its interpretation.

During his teenage years he studied in Avignon where his fascination with both astronomy and astrology was probably further nurtured and his understanding expanded. Nostradamus is known to have subscribed enthusiastically to Copernicus' theories which included the radical understanding that the earth revolved around the sun, its orbit conjoined with the movement of other members of the planetary system. He was also, however, developing a wider and potentially dangerous interest in the magic arts. Avignon, at that time, appears to have possessed a fine library collection of scholarly astrological and occult books and so concerned was his family that this burgeoning preoccupation with the occult might bring him to the attention of a hostile officialdom that in 1522

he was sent to the University of Montpellier to study medicine. He obtained his *baccalauréat* there in 1525. It must have been from amongst these raw ingredients that he fashioned the prognostications and the system of dating which he managed so adroitly to hide from the world at large.

Nostradamus' interest became focused on treatment of the plague. He was born into an era bedevilled by two great social evils, one of which was the lethal bacterium, *Pasteurella pestis*, which had first struck Europe in 1348 as the Black Death. During the sixteenth century the disease was virtually endemic in southern France where it was known popularly as 'le charbon'. He worked as an itinerant doctor and there are notes that he practised in Narbonne, Carcassonne, Toulouse and Bordeaux before returning to Avignon and from there to Montpellier to further his studies in medicine. But he fell foul of conventional understanding that the plague, in company with fire, was inflicted as some measure of divine retribution on humanity. Ahead of his time he seems to have half-guessed how the disease was transmitted and he promoted simple antiseptic procedures and herbal therapies to the extent that, by 1525, he had gained a local reputation as a healer. He refused to adopt the conventional, and wholly ineffectual, methods of treatment including bleeding with leeches and his unorthodox approach generated considerable suspicion amongst other physicians who more or less accused him of witchcraft. The result was

THE BLACK DEATH OF 1348 IS STRIKINGLY VISUALIZED IN THIS ILLUSTRATION OF THE DEATH OF LAURA TAKEN FROM AN EDITION OF THE POETRY OF PETRARCH OF 1503.

that he returned to his nomadic existence as a wandering scholarly physician.

At some stage he was befriended by a celebrated Italian philosopher and humanist, Julius César Scalinger (1484–1558) who wrote several commentaries on the classical writers and who is probably best known for his controversial attacks on fellow humanist Erasmus. Nostradamus went to live with Scalinger in the town of Agen where, in about 1534, he married for the first time. His wife bore him two children but the marriage was destined to end in tragedy. In spite of Nostradamus' radical attempts to deal with the plague all three succumbed and no record of their names has survived. Their deaths appeared to trigger a series of misfortunes commencing with a legal action instigated by his dead wife's family for the return of her dowry. Nostradamus fell out with Scalinger and then was accused of heresy, ironically because detractors elected to report a minor incident that has occurred several years earlier when Nostradamus had been overheard to observe critically that a newly erected bronze statue of the Virgin Mary was of diabolical quality. On learning that the ecclesiastical authorities in Toulouse were about to apply for his attendance before the Inquisition, Nostradamus made a judicious withdrawal

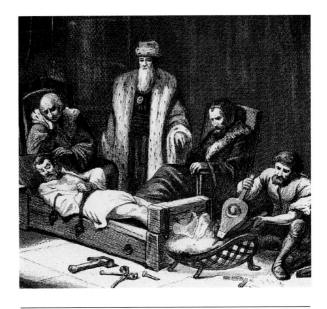

A NINETEENTH-CENTURY ENGRAVING DEPICTS SOME OF THE HORRORS OF THE INQUISITION, A FEARED BUT NOT UNFAMILIAR FEATURE OF SIXTEENTH-CENTURY LIFE.

and set off once more on his itinerant lifestyle. This time he travelled further afield, visiting Italy, and it was there that his powers of prophecy first seem to have taken root.

In about 1554 he returned to France and took up residence in the plague-ridden environs of the southern port of Marseilles. Based there he redoubled his efforts to save the sick and dying in the Provençal region, including the city of Aix. He settled eventually in the town of Salon where he bought a house and married for the second time. His wife, Anne Ponsart Gemelle, who was herself a widow of some affluence, bore him a number of children including the son, César, to whom the prophetic works were entrusted, and it was in Salon that he began compiling almanacs and, eventually, the *quatrains*.

When writing his predictions the first concern of Nostradamus was, undoubtedly, for his own safety and that of his family. The threat came from two quarters. The terrible endemic disease against which he fought so courageously as a plague doctor was matched in its singularity of purpose by the Church in her zeal against what was perceived as a not unrelated disease of society, that of heresy and witchcraft. The slightest hint reaching the ears of the ecclesiastical authorities that Nostradamus was dabbling in the magic arts might have resulted in his arraignment before the Papal Inquisition, the formal court of enquiry established during the thirteenth century by the

JULIUS CÉSAR SCALINGER, A CELEBRATED DOCTOR AND PHILOSOPHER, WAS A CONTEMPORARY OF NOSTRADAMUS AND FOR SOME TIME SHARED HIS HOME WITH THE SEER.

THE BURNING OF THREE WITCHES IN THE HARZ MOUNTAINS OF GERMANY DRAMATICALLY ILLUSTRATES HOW THE THREAT OF PERSECUTION LED NOSTRADAMUS TO COUCH HIS PREDICTIONS IN ENIGMATIC TERMS.

Catholic Church following the crusade to quash the Catharist heresy in southern France. The witchcraft that was subject to extensive persecution in Europe during the sixteenth century was carried out by persons who applied innate or self-raised powers of magic to dispense forces for good or evil purposes. There was no special distinction between benevolent and malevolent magicians and so charges, designed to enforce legal sanctions against witches and heretics, could technically have been brought had any of Nostradamus' prophecies been revealed by subsequent events to be accurate.

There would have been severe consequences had any of the more damaging predictions come to pass since the cause of misfortune, attributed to the seer, would have been classified as *maleficium*, the Latin legal term defining harm wrought on other members of society by a witch or sorcerer, one which frequently became linked with diabolism and which, if proven, carried the death penalty. That he went in fear of gossip and local superstition is indicated by an ugly incident when the people of Salon burnt his effigy outside his house and he found it necessary to plead protection from no lesser

personage than the Queen, Catherine de Medici. There is a particular irony in this since Nostradamus had already made predictions which appeared to relate adversely to her husband and her children and which therefore constituted precisely the kind of dark omens that could, technically, have jeopardized his safety and that of his family.

Nostradamus' association with the French Queen is a curious one and it is difficult to know how much is genuine and how much is apocryphal, attributable to popular rumour. There are indications that Catherine went so far as to visit him in Salon on at least one occasion. This occurred during the Royal Progress of 1564 after she had become Regent of France to oversee the minority of her second son, Charles IX. Given that, at the time, Nostradamus was in a degree of fear for his own safety and the fact that the Queen both bestowed on him the title Physician in the Ordinary and provided him with an annual salary must have given him some relief from his oppressors.

Earlier, in July or August 1556, Catherine had sent for Nostradamus at a time when the first of his prophecies had already been published and were the subject of intense speculation at the French court. Her chief

IN A POPULAR PRINT, NOSTRADAMUS USES A MAGIC MIRROR TO
REVEAL TO THE QUEEN, CATHERINE DE MEDICI, THE TRAGIC
FATE OF HER CHILDREN.

concern is said to have been the prophetic warning
contained in *CI, Q35* hinting at the death of her husband,
Henri II:

> *Le lyon jeune le vieux surmontera*
> *En champ bellique par singulier duelle*
> *Dans caige d'or les yeux luy crevera*
> *Deux classes une, puis mourir, mort cruelle.*

> *The young lion will vanquish the elder one, in single*
> *combat on the battlefield: he will pierce the eyes in their*
> *golden cage; two wounds in one, thence to meet a cruel*
> *death.*

Henri II had already been warned by another seer that his
reign would be marked, at the opening and close, by
personal combat. In the event the prophecies became

CATHERINE DE MEDICI, WIFE OF HENRI II OF FRANCE,
ATTACHED GREAT IMPORTANCE TO THE WORDS OF
NOSTRADAMUS.

horribly true since Henri was destined to be killed by a lance which fatally penetrated his gilded helmet in lists during the summer of 1559. His opponent would be the young Montgomery, Captain of the Scottish Guard.

It is said that in whichever way Nostradamus assured the Queen concerning the *quatrain*, she believed him and provided him with a small reward for his services. Subsequently Catherine asked him to prepare horoscopes for her seven children and it seems that she effectively accepted him as her protégé despite the fact that he had also already predicted their tragic fate.

Henri II died, in circumstances too close to the prediction in **CI, Q35** to give Nostradamus any sense of security from the ecclesiastical authorities and he decided to delay publication of further material beyond that which was already being circulated in more elite circles. In fact the completed works were destined not to be printed until two years after his death.

Nostradamus died in 1566 at the age of 62, probably from kidney failure, and was buried at Salon. In later years, during the French Revolution, his tomb was desecrated by superstitious soldiers. They managed to scatter his mortal remains before the mayor of the town ordered them to be collected and reinterred in the church of Saint-Laurent where they remain to this day. The epitaph on Nostradamus' tomb reads:

> *Here lie the bones of the illustrious Michel Nostradamus,*
> *whose near divine pen was alone, in the judgement of all mortals,*
> *worthy to record under the inspiration of the stars,*
> *the future events of the whole world . . .*
> *posterity invade not his rest.*

Insurance and Inspiration

Nostradamus might well have been mindful of the caution exercised by his Polish contemporary Nicolaus Copernicus in promoting radical ideas which could be attacked on grounds of heresy. Only amongst a few trusted friends was Copernicus able to circulate his outrageous theory that the earth orbited the sun as part of a solar system, since

AN ILLUSTRATION OF THE ZODIAC AS DEVISED BY COPERNICUS, IN WHICH THE EARTH IS SHOWN TO ORBIT THE SUN.

his findings clashed severely with the Church's claim that the earth was at the centre of the universe.

Aside from the insurance provided by his royal protector, Nostradamus' precautions to safeguard himself took a different course. Whilst he was content to have some of the prophecies published during his lifetime and in his own country, appearing under the title of *Centuries*, his insurance came in the method by which he couched most of the *quatrains* in such thoroughly obscure terms. By the simple but effective device of making the *quatrains* open to liberal inventiveness in their interpretation and avoiding firm calendar dates, he made predictions that could not be linked, with any degree of certainty, to future events, persons or places.

If a code exists, and one must assume in this respect that Nostradamus was not merely playing a cruel joke on future generations, then logically the code was contrived out of his personal experience and training. Nostradamus' abiding interest remained within the occult sciences of his day – astrology, hermeticism and necromancy and the fascination did not decline during his years as a physician. From the limited details available it appears that his pursuit of the magic arts truly took flight in about 1527 when, as a young man of 24, he returned for a time to Avignon and its occult library as a respite from working among the sick and dying in plague-ridden Bordeaux.

Clues to the content of the prophecies may lie, to an extent, in the type of esoteric books which Nostradamus relied on as the foundation of his divinatory techniques. It has been alleged that he subsequently burned many of

THE GODDESS HATHOR PLACES A MAGIC COLLAR ON SETI I, IN THE NINETEENTH DYNASTY OF THE EGYPTIAN KINGS. NOSTRADAMUS WAS GREATLY INTERESTED IN EGYPTIAN OCCULTISM.

these because he feared that they might open a pathway to his own secrets, although the claims about their disposal are unsubstantiated.

There is some indication that he was schooled in the occult elements of the Jewish mystery tradition contained in the *Qabalah* and it is significant that one of the most important commentators on the Qabalistic texts was Nostradamus' contemporary, Isaac Luria (1534–72), the Jewish mystic who founded a significant school of Qabalah at Safed in Galilee. The message of the *Qabalah* is that the creation of the world was achieved through a series of emanations, the ten *sefirot* dispensed by God, and that these provide the essence of all reality in which a flow of energy sustains both mankind and nature. In use, the *Qabalah* consists of a number of branched and connecting pathways which form a complex pattern not unlike a 'Cat's Cradle' and referred to as the Tree of Life.

From the fifteenth century onwards, many Christian European occultists had relied on the teachings of the *Qabalah* in order to pursue their interest in hermeticism. This intellectual approach to magic, reliant on a mix of astrological and alchemical principles, first arose in Renaissance Italy and was based on the translation of the classical Greek manuscript, *Corpus Hermeticum*. This treatise proposed that it was possible for humankind to regain the control, lost by Adam at the Fall, over the natural world in both present and future.

Nostradamus was also deeply interested in Egyptian occultism. An assortment of textbooks on the subject were available in France during the sixteenth century and there is reasonable evidence that he relied heavily on at least one of them, the work entitled *De Mysteriis Egyptorum*, an imprint of which was published in Lyon in 1547. Some of the prophecies appear to draw on its writing, more or less line for line.

It was, however, in the machinery of astrology that Nostradamus' interest lay most strongly and from 1550 onwards he was producing a yearly almanac. The publication of astrological forecasts in the form of almanacs had become enormously popular amongst ordinary people by Nostradamus' time. One of the French forerunners produced at the end of the fifteenth century was a pocket edition which, when it became translated into English in 1503, was titled *The Kalendar of Shepherdes*. Although those almanacs originating in France and Italy led the way, in England alone it is reckoned that over six hundred had been published before 1600 and the *Kalendar of Shepherdes* is thought to have been reprinted at least 17 times in English before the mid 1600s. Most almanacs were sold out almost as soon as they appeared but they were not universally well received. It was largely their success which also made them the butt of criticism in certain quarters since the forecasts could lead to personal loss as well as gain.

The standard almanac was sold in three parts and included the actual Almanac of astronomical events for the coming year such as eclipses, conjunctions and movable feasts, the Kalendar with such details as days of the week and month and church festivals, and the Prognostication which contained an astrological forecast of the notable events of the year ahead.

The more comprehensive almanacs also contained tables known as Ephemerides which showed the positions of the heavenly bodies for the different days of the year. By referring to these tables the reader could chart the positions of the planets in relation to the star constellations of the Zodiac. This permitted analysis of the various conjunctions and oppositions and provided a basis upon which the author made his predictions for the year ahead. These would generally include such details as the weather, the quality of the harvest and the general health of the population, but would also introduce elements of a political nature. Any change in the heavens was particularly seized upon as a significant portent of events to come, and when such changes were seen the almanacs were pored over for advice and prognostication. Events

such as the emergence of a new star in the constellation of Cassiopeia in 1572 and a comet which appeared in 1577 were regarded by king and commoner alike as outstanding premonitory signs.

Often the almanacs were produced by men working in the field of medicine and carried advertisements for books and patent remedies. One of the best known in England is that of Francis Moore (1675–1715), now known as *Old Moore's Almanac*, which was effectively founded in order to promote his proprietary brands of medicine. Nostradamus' almanacs were no less popular in France and must be seen as a prelude to the publication of his books of prophecies.

It is improbable that the dating system used in the *quatrains* stems from two of Nostradamus' interests – necromancy and alchemy. Necromancy, in particular, is a term little understood in the twentieth century. It was not, generally, applied as a divinatory technique but was considered by a limited number of individuals to be an adjunct to magical arts of a fairly dubious nature. During the sixteenth century, skulls, parts of corpses and

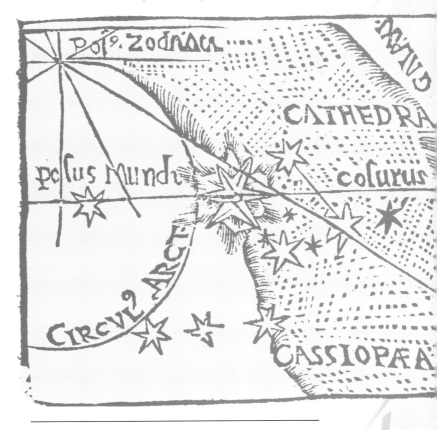

CORNELIUS GEMMA'S DEPICTION OF A NEW STAR IN CASSIOPEIA IN 1572: SUCH EVENTS WERE WIDELY REGARDED AS PREMONITORY SIGNS.

graveyard earth were employed occasionally for magical purposes. Certain quack healers known as 'strokers', for example, followed the revolting practice of lifting sufferers from various diseases to be touched by the hand of a newly hanged felon. Others relied on concoctions made from rotting corpses and offered their clients brews from skulls. The use of body parts for serious divination was limited and by and large the necromancers were individuals either on the fringes of society or those desperate to alleviate poverty. Sometimes they were students, too poor to maintain themselves at university, who saw a means of raising cash. It is, therefore, possible that the young Nostradamus dabbled in the art of necromancy for a while but it seems unlikely that he drew on it much in later life when writing his prophecies.

Neither was alchemy a factor in the making of predictions and the only tenuous link between it and astrology lies in that the latter provided a choice of times that were important for conducting alchemical operations, largely focused on attempts to turn base metals into gold

and on preparing elixirs. Astrology already provided similar guidance indicating the times for gathering of magical herbs and conjuration of spirits. Alchemy was not an aid to astrology, rather astrology assisted alchemy.

It seems reasonable to guess that the code lies with astrology coupled with an understanding of mathematics and, perhaps, of the Jewish *Qabalah*. Since Nostradamus was not celebrated as a mathematician it may also be assumed that the maths employed was of a fairly straightforward nature. Suggestions that the dating code relies on mathematical formulae of such complex nature that modern computer applications are unable to decipher them are frankly ludicrous.

Clearly the code was only of use if it could be read, at least by a selected audience, but it is equally certain that Michel de Notredame did not intend to offer the Church's Commission of Inquiry any scope to detect his secrets once the material was published. In other words, the secret of the code had to conform to certain prerequisites which would make it available, with a little

AN ALCHEMIST'S LABORATORY IN THE SIXTEENTH CENTURY.

imagination and insight, to those of sympathetic disposition whilst leaving the ecclesiastical authorities nonplussed. To suggest that the code was so secretive and so complex that it was impossible to decipher could only mean that this otherwise astute and forward-thinking man failed in the most important aspect of his labours – to communicate his visions for the benefit of future generations of humanity.

The Letter

When Nostradamus realized, in 1566, that his life was coming to a close he entrusted the text of the prophecies, without much doubt unfinished, to his young son, César, with an accompanying letter written from Salon and dated 1 March 1555. There is no indication that he communicated with César on the subject of the predictions other than in that famous letter which now forms the preface to the first complete edition, and it is clear from the content of the letter that the father intended the son not only to read but to *understand* the prophecies. In this child he must have considered that he had a safe and understanding executor.

Nostradamus begins with a clear statement of intent: *Your late arrival, César Notredame, my son, has made me spend much time in constant nightly reflection so that I could communicate with you by letter and leave you this reminder, after my death, for the benefit of all men.*

The letter is composed with great love and candour to a boy still too young to understand the words, yet some authors have gone so far as to insist that it was penned in an obscure code known only to members of an elite hermetic society of which father and son were both initiates. This, it is claimed, allowed them to communicate in a covert manner and for César to have the means at his disposal for decoding the chronological sequence and dating of the *quatrains*. Yet there is not the slightest indication of such a secret liaison and the proposal, once again, drifts into the realms of bizarre fantasy.

On the contrary, Nostradamus is open about several aspects. He tells César that *the key to the code is locked inside my heart* but he also advises that it will take his son not years but merely months to understand the work which has been made obscure only to confound *the injustice of the age*, a term by which he refers to the bigotry

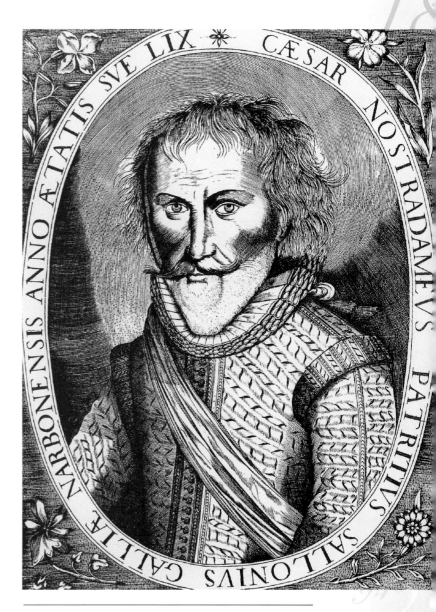

CÉSAR, NOSTRADAMUS' SON AND RECIPIENT OF THE FAMOUS LETTER WHICH ACCOMPANIED HIS FATHER'S MOMENTOUS TEXTS.

of the Church. He also reveals that the prophecies constitute *what the divine spirit has vouchsafed me to know by means of astronomy* and he goes on to reinforce the opinion that his visionary ability is obtained through a combination of received images and orthodox astrology which he refers to as *contemplation of the distant stars as if in vigil*. This reliance on inspired revelation and astral science is repeated several times in the content of the letter and is reinforced in the way that the volumes of prophecies are constructed. Each volume is referred to as a Century but it should be made clear that these are not centuries of years, rather of prophecies, since each complete Century comprises 100 *quatrains*. The astrological basis of prediction seems to be indicated by the fact that Nostradamus proposed to divide the work into twelve parts, the number of astral constellations in the Zodiac. There has been some suggestion that the twelve sections are to be equated with the Labours of Hercules but only, it seems, because of a passing reference in the letter to César concerning 'Herculean efforts'.

Conventional analysis suggests that Nostradamus intended to write ten Centuries, but then commenced work on two more as an afterthought and was prevented from completing them by his death. This explanation, however, is not wholly convincing because several of the Centuries, not merely the eleventh and twelfth, are incomplete. Century VII, for example, includes only 46 *quatrains*, Century XI has a mere two and Century XII includes 11 predictions. The clear inference from this is that Nostradamus did not compile the predictions sequentially from Century I to XII but rather that he worked on various Centuries concurrently and in no particular order. Appreciation of this has a considerable impact on the interpretation of the work.

Nostradamus also introduces a caveat which many would-be interpreters have ignored at their peril. He writes of *future events which cannot be understood merely through being revealed. Neither can they be grasped through men's interpretations nor through another mode of cognizance ... neither in the present nor in the total eternity to come.* Too many investigators are ready to ignore this warning. Hence Jean-Charles de Fontbrune makes the error of asserting confidently that the prophecies of Nostradamus were *written in the sixteenth century in order to depict the twentieth, to which two-thirds of the work is devoted, for their author seemed to know that his text would be expounded and understood only in the century which was the focus of his vision.* The statement presumes a great deal and is wholly speculative. It relies on a form of chronological reckoning recorded in a separate letter to *Henry Roy de France Second* but even this requires considerable mathematical juggling to arrive at the conclusions drawn by de Fontbrune concerning dates.

A HIGHLY DECORATED ZODIAC FROM LALLEMANT DE BETZ.

Aquarius
Balena
Pisces Austrinus
Phœnix
Fluvius
Orion
Lepus
Taurus
Lang
Nubecula
Dorado
Hydrus
Polus Antarc
Apous
Canis maior
Gemini
Argo Navis
Canicula
Cancer
Centaurus
Hydra
Crater
Leo
Equator
Corvus
Virgo

Nostradamus left to César a mass of material written in what he himself describes as a nebulous rather than plainly prophetic form. Yet we must assume that César, when mature enough, would have the means at his disposal to understand its content. It has been suggested that the books of reference which Nostradamus elected to destroy by burning were the sole key to decipherment, yet to what purpose did he eliminate them if the legacy thereby became meaningless? Why would Nostradamus leave to his son something which was destined to remain useless without a comprehensive library, from many different disciplines, which one must presume César did not have at his disposal from any other source? One of the most revealing comments comes at the close of the letter: *Take this gift from your father M. Nostradamus who hopes you will understand each prophecy in every* quatrain *herein.* This is surely not the sentiment of a man who intends to present his son and heir only with volumes of unintelligible riddles.

Nostradamus provided, occasionally, something very much at odds with the nebulous style. This unusual element is not immediately discernible since it has been embedded in a scattered, almost random fashion within the prophecies and the letter to César. The reader is obliged to work through the texts painstakingly but, by the end, certain details have emerged which are far from being of a vague nature. The outcome is reminiscent of the long and complicated algebraic formula in the midst of which is a single numerical figure, or the enigma crossword puzzle with neither numbers nor black squares completed except for a single answer. It is these details which stand out in stark, almost shocking contrast to the nebulous nature of the rest. Nostradamus has introduced details that are so precise and carefully defined, they can only be treated as starting points from which to break the code.

This inclusion of detail occurs in very few places, twice in the letter to César and once or twice in the *quatrains*. The letter, which forms the preface to the *Centuries* in the 1568 imprint, was undoubtedly penned as an intimate communication from father to son and was presumably never intended for wider publication and its dating, 1 March 1555, must be regarded as significant in itself. Amongst its advice, the letter explains, using an exact numerical figure, that the work comprises

prophecies until the year 3797 CE. It has been proposed by certain authors that this dating represents another deliberate deception based on the Judaic timescale from the beginning of biblical creation to the birth of Christ. The biblical chronology is calculated in a prose synopsis at the close of *CVII* as being 4757 years, to which has been added the 2242 year span between the time of writing until 3797, making 6999 years, less the pre-Christian era which suddenly becomes translated as 4000 years, leaving a closing date of 1999 CE.

Another analyst of Nostradamus, Peter Lemesurier, bases his calculation on a wide list of sources, from the Great Pyramid of Giza, through Hindu and Buddhist scriptures, to Nostradamus himself and advises, in an aptly titled work, *Nostradamus – the Final Reckoning* that 'the overall sequence of major future events has already been mapped out from 1995 until at least the year 4000'. The problem with this argument is that we have no indication that César, even if he could understand their deeper meaning, had access to such occult and exotic sources. César's chief claim to fame is a work entitled *Histoire de Provence* (1614). Lemesurier indicates that his own account of Nostradamus' predictions is dramatic but not *melo*dramatic sparing 'the usual sensationalist scenarios of virtually unmitigated universal doom' whilst 'imposing no preconceived agendas', but then he predicts 'the coming Islamic invasion and virtual destruction of southern and western Europe, the siege and bombardment of Britain, the long-delayed western counter-attack, an ensuing age of peace and plenty, an era of renewed cataclysm and decline, eventual extraterrestrial saviours and the ultimate transformation of humanity'.

Aside from the very reasonable question of why Nostradamus would generate such a piece of intrigue in a letter which was otherwise composed with considerable candour, it offers a mathematically inconvenient and equally unconvincing argument since the permutation wholly ignores the 1555 years which elapsed between the birth of Christ and the year of the letter. If properly added to the account this would generate a closing date of 8554 CE.

The second date is to be found elsewhere in the letter. Here Nostradamus includes a precision that might seem ludicrous to the casual observer. He identifies that, according to astronomical calculations and from the time of writing to César, in exactly 177 years, 3 months and 11 days, the Golden Age shall return.

A third detail relating to the dating is found within the *quatrains*. In **CX, Q72** he reveals that an event of particular importance will take place in France in July 1999.

One of the major misunderstandings which has been promoted by several writers lies in the unsubstantiated claim that Nostradamus deliberately confused the time sequences of the prophecies so that their dating arrangement would not be revealed to the uninitiated. This assumption is based, however, on the inaccurate reading of an important observation towards the close of his letter to César. He mentions that he has compiled certain material in a non-chronological sequence but he is not referring, in this context, to the poetically constructed *quatrains*. Rather he is describing the other prophecies, the 141 *présages* or portents, composed *in soluta oratione*, in other words in prose. He qualifies this by saying: 'I have limited the places and times and exact dates so that future generations will see, whilst experiencing these inevitable events, how I have listed others in clearer language, so that despite their obscurities, these things shall be understood.'

When considering these dates a cautionary note has to be introduced. Nostradamus lived in a time when the old Julian calendar was still in use throughout the Christian world. It was not replaced by the more accurate Gregorian version until 1582. The Julian calendar, established by Julius Caesar in 46 BCE, was flawed in that it ran behind the solar calendar. It included three years, each of 365 days, followed by a leap year of 366 and the leap years had too great a frequency. This resulted in the calendar gaining an extra day about every 128 years. Over the centuries it had developed a cumulative inaccuracy so that, by the sixteenth century, when Pope Gregory applied the simple

JULIUS CAESAR ESTABLISHED THE JULIAN CALENDAR IN 46 BCE, THE PRECURSOR OF OUR DATING SYSTEM.

expedient of adding an appropriate number of days to the nominal date, it was running ten days fast. Futuristic predictions made prior to 1582 did not take this aberration into account and may need to be adjusted accordingly.

There are other misconceptions arising from the letter which tend to have been instigated by one and then slavishly followed by various Nostradamus-watchers. These include the reference which Nostradamus makes, early in the letter, to *le commun advenement*, the 'Vulgar Advent'. It has been interpreted by commentators as being a

POPE GREGORY XIII WAS RESPONSIBLE FOR AMENDING THE JULIAN CALENDAR TO BRING IT IN LINE WITH THE SOLAR CALENDAR – HENCE THE GREGORIAN CALENDAR IN USE TODAY.

reference to republicanism via the French revolution and then to its development towards and change into communism. But the concept of the republic, in the sense of an accession to power by the people, was not the innovative property of France in the eighteenth century whereby, in 1793, the National Convention proclaimed a republic and executed Louis XVI. The concept of the republic is considerably older. It was effectively launched by the Roman writer Plato and constitutes the title of, arguably, his best-known work. It is worth noting that the term 'republican' was also incorporated by Thomas Jefferson in 1792 when he formed the party of Republican Democrats in America.

These, therefore, are the basic elements from which any successful detection of Nostradamus' key needs to proceed. But in order to do so it is essential to wipe the slate clean of any preconceived notions, many of which have been relied on in the recent past to 'decipher' the prophecies.

The Millennium Scenario

If there is a single feature amongst Nostradamus-watchers which serves to bind two schools of otherwise contrasting comprehension, style and output, it is the lure of the apocalyptic 'millennium' scenario. Yet this crisis for humanity has been widely misinterpreted and the fundamental failure to understand the sense of the term 'millennium' has been largely responsible for the lurid interest in disaster predictions occurring before, during and after the close of the twentieth century.

It is essential, when trying to make sense of Nostradamus' predictions, to understand what was meant by 'the millennium' and by the vision of an ultimate apocalypse, Armageddon, heralding the Second Coming and the Day of Judgement. Most of this grim scenario is drawn from the New Testament Book of Revelation.

And there were voices, and thunders, and lightnings; and there was a great earthquake, such as was not since men were upon the earth, so mighty an earthquake and so great. And the great city was divided into three parts, and the cities of the nations fell: and great Babylon came into remembrance before God, to give unto her the cup of the wine of the fierceness of his wrath. And every island fled away, and the mountains were not found. And

there fell upon men a great hail out of heaven ... and I saw the heaven opened, and behold a white horse; and he that sat upon him was called Faithful and True, and in righteousness he doth judge and make war. (REV. 16:18ff. and 19:11).

This imagery was dreamed up in a bygone political climate, more than a thousand years before the time of Nostradamus, when people were yearning for and anticipating the restoration of the Israelite kingdom, in Syrio-Palestine, in a welter of blood and retribution headed by a resurrected Messiah. Jesus Christ himself believed passionately in a new kingdom for the Jews and preached of its imminent arrival. His viewpoint was strongly apocalyptic in that the existing order would end, and in its place would come a new heaven on earth with the down-trodden faithful entitled to a prominent and favoured position. Armageddon was envisaged not so much as an event but a place where, according to *Revelation* 16:14, on an unspecified date the agents of the Devil will do battle with God Almighty.

The battle to end all battles was to have a prelude in the shape of a series of disasters for humanity, the vivid imagery once again fuelled from *The Book of Revelation*:

And I saw, and behold a white horse and he that sat on him had a bow; and a crown was given unto him; and he went forth conquering and to conquer ... and there went out another horse that was red; and power was given to him that sat thereon to take peace from the earth, and that they should kill one another; and there was given unto him a great sword ... and I beheld, and lo a black horse; and he that sat on him had a pair of balances in his hand ... and I looked, and behold a pale horse; and his name that sat on him was death, and hell followed with him. And power was given unto them over the fourth part of the earth, to kill with sword, and with hunger, and with death, and with the beasts of the earth.

The evocative words of Revelation 6 concerning the Four Horsemen of the Apocalypse have tantalized biblical

ALBRECHT DÜRER'S INTERPRETATION OF THE VIVID WORDS OF REVELATION CHAPTER 6, WHOSE IMAGES ARE KNOWN AS THE FOUR HORSEMEN OF THE APOCALYPSE.

BELIEF IN THE DAY OF JUDGEMENT WAS WIDESPREAD IN NOSTRADAMUS' TIME, AS DEMONSTRATED IN THIS
FIFTEENTH-CENTURY RUSSIAN PAINTING.

fundamentalists and prophets of doom throughout the Christian era. Their impact has never waned and the appearance of the Horsemen has been a subject of intense interest amongst seers, carriers of placards, great artists and post-war cinema directors alike.

In the immediate aftermath of Christ's death, there were those in the newly fledged Christian movement who found such proclamations vaguely embarrassing and very shortly, as the idea lost serious credibility, the urgent anticipation of the apocalypse was quietly dropped by the early Christian fathers. Yet by Nostradamus' time the belief in Armageddon and an imminent Day of Judgement when Christ would 'come to judge the quick and the dead', in the guise of some dreadful avenging colossus, was again widespread and fashionable. General interest in prophecy was, as has been explained, extensive and Nostradamus was not alone in his abilities. Such dreams provided men with authority and were often used to persuade others of the correctness of their theories or actions.

The term 'millennium', which in purely chronological terms refers to a period of 1000 years, has been frequently misrepresented by those sensation-minded authors anxious to prove that the main thrust of Nostradamus' predictions relate to the latter part of the twentieth century. Theirs, however, is not the way in which millennium was understood in sixteenth-century Christian Europe because the medieval theologians and philosophers took it to mean not the *end* of an era but the *beginning*. It represented a minimum of 1000 years when Christ and his saints would return to rule the earth in peace and harmony. Attention eventually shifted away from the immediacy of the Second Coming but this change of view did not come about until the eighteenth century. Meanwhile medieval Europe witnessed a proliferation of prophets and fortune-tellers from all social classes who believed that the millennium was *imminent*. Much of the popular interest resulted from the increased availability of the Bible to common people, whereas before it had been restricted to the clergy and the aristocracy. The books of Daniel and Revelation were eagerly read and digested and the most widely predicted date for Armageddon was 1666 since the 'great beast' of Revelation had been given the name '666'.

The advent of the apocalypse was also linked to a separate prediction by John the Divine, that Armageddon will be presaged by the appearance of the antichrist, some terrible agent of the Devil and his forces of darkness.

Little children, it is the last time; and as ye have heard that antichrist shall come, even now are there many antichrists; whereby we know that it is the last time. (1 JOHN 2:18)

In the minds of many sixteenth-century philosophers the antichrist was already in place. For some it had come in the form of the plague, for others it was represented by the darkness of papal supremacy. For English Catholics it had manifested itself in the guise of the Protestant Queen Elizabeth

There was, and still is, particular interest in prophecies, including the *quatrains* of Nostradamus, which appear to predict major political and military upheavals. Interest in foretelling the exact date of the millennium was particularly strong amongst minority groups and radicals, and Nostradamus qualified in both of these categories. Although his family had converted to Catholicism he was of Semitic stock and still suffering the social stigma of being a Jew in a climate steeped in religious bigotry. His parents had raised him in the Catholic faith more out of political and social expediency

ADOLF HITLER AS ANTICHRIST? THIS WAS THE VIEW PUT FORWARD IN THE 1930S BY MAX DE FONTBRUNE.

than any realignment of belief. He was also advocating radical medical treatments which were regarded with great suspicion amongst his fellow peers. One should not lose sight of the fact that Nostradamus' interest in prophecy was, to some degree, motivated by self-interest.

Nostradamus made it clear that the present age, as he saw it, would end in a massive conflagration or holocaust. He wrote of the millennium in apocalyptic terms with much reference to war, fiery missiles falling from the sky and great floods and it makes dramatic reading if he can be interpreted to have foreseen terrible happenings taking place in the immediate decades around the end of the twentieth century. This facile analysis, however, wholly disregards the political, social and religious climate in which Nostradamus lived and with which we have no reason to believe he was out of step.

Even those who now dismiss the scenario in which the Soviet empire unleashes war on the west, have managed to replace this dreadful prognosis with one, no less appalling, whereby Europe will be invaded in the year 2000 by combined forces of Asiatic hordes and Islamic fundamentalists.

Nostradamus was undoubtedly influenced by the Book of Revelation but to interpret his more gloomy predictions as referring to our immediate era is to disregard the reality of the culture in which he lived. The catastrophic event which Nostradamus describes as 'the millennium' is wholly misinterpreted if it is taken to be the end of a thousand-year period culminating in 1999.

He makes reference to the return of the 'Golden Age'. This is generally understood to mean the new Age of Aquarius when the wrongs of the current era will be resolved (according to Revelation through war, pestilence, famine and death) and will give way to a new and better world. But the dawn of the Age of Aquarius is not projected as taking place in 1999 even by most modern astrologers who consider that the Age will begin 'sometime' *during* the next millennium. Nostradamus unequivocally foresaw the 'new dawn' as taking place accountably earlier. In his letter to César he identified the 'countdown' to the event, specifically, as coming after 177 years after 1555. This places its start in 1732 CE.

Modern writers have conveniently overlooked the pronouncement, however, and been determined to search

for antichrists as harbingers of Armageddon in our own lifetimes. It is of interest that, in 1938, Max de Fontbrune published a major commentary on the prophecies which placed Hitler as the 'antichrist', concentrated much attention on the impending German military advance through the low countries and predicted the disastrous outcome of the war for the Third Reich. This earned the unfavourable attentions of the Gestapo and the book was withdrawn from sale, its copies confiscated and destroyed.

By and large, though, in recent decades the focus has been directed to the auspicious date of 1999 for some all-consuming catastrophic event to occur. It is not altogether surprising that most modern Nostradamus-watchers have willingly seized on the same 'selling point'. They have interpreted key *quatrains* to reveal that Nostradamus foresaw a decidedly messy end for humanity, or at least a sizeable portion of it, occurring sometime around the year 2000.

Our most favoured demise, heralded by such lurid and eye-catching titles as *Nostradamus — Countdown to*

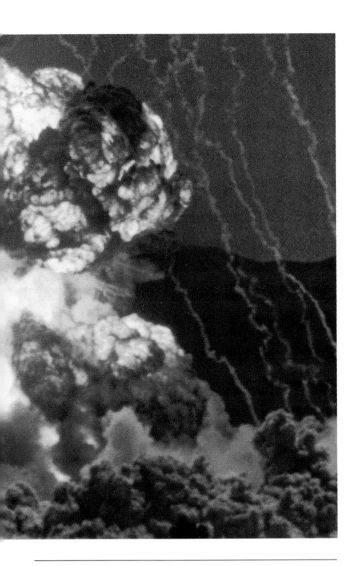

MANY NOSTRADAMUS-WATCHERS HAVE SOUGHT TO LINK PREDICTIONS OF APOCALYPSE WITH THE DESTRUCTION OF THE WORLD IN A NUCLEAR EXPLOSION, DESPITE THE FACT THAT NOSTRADAMUS KNEW NOTHING OF SS20 MISSILES!

Apocalypse and *Nostradamus – the Final Reckoning*, takes place when World War Three is triggered and we disappear into a collective cloud of atomic vapour during a nuclear holocaust delivered by the 'opposition', or are quenched by Islamic hordes who resort to biological warfare, backed by some Asiatic warlord, in their conquest of Europe.

If one happens to be interested in Nostradamus and lives in the western world, then the perpetrators of this impending catastrophe tend to stem either from the old Soviet bloc or China, or include some deranged Middle Eastern despot determined that Islam shall rule over the contaminated ruins of civilization. On the other hand, Nostradamus-watchers in Russia, China and the more militant and fundamentalist Islamic regimes will search

the *quatrains* for clues to an Armageddon triggered from the capitalist west and steered by the 'Great Satan' in the collective guise of the United States of America.

This 'End of the World' scenario, involving worldwide catastrophe is an extremely old 'chestnut' which has caused considerable embarrassment not merely in the early centuries of Christendom but throughout the history of the Christian Church, especially when 'the ultimate horror' has not materialized on the date prescribed. Nonetheless we have regurgitated it as a matter of stubborn routine and, with equal regularity, been found wanting in our predictions. The history of modern cults, including Seventh Day Adventists, Plymouth Brethren, Jehovah's Witnesses and others, is peppered with eccentric and colourful characters proclaiming that 'doom is nigh'. Jehovah's Witnesses have found the threat of Judgement Day – usually not too far distant – to be the most persuasive tool with which to recruit new members. Recent options have included 1914, 1925 and 1975. It is worth noting, however, that the leaders of the Witnesses announced in November 1995 that, owing to earlier miscalculations, they were no longer able to predict the date of Armageddon.

Nostradamus has proved an enduring source of predictive fodder which refers to the decades approaching the millennium. Yet in spite of our keenness to find the portents of our own twentieth-century doom in his writings, often accompanied by the dubious mathematical juggling through which we arrive at their place in the calendar, it is becoming increasingly difficult to attach credence to dire predictions of events taking place within the next few years. Writing in 1984, de Fontbrune described a Soviet invasion of Britain which would take place in the 1990s followed by nuclear destruction in 1999, probably emanating from further east. But by 1992 the Warsaw Pact had disintegrated and when we turn to later writers, such as Peter Lemesurier, whose work *Nostradamus – the next 50 years* was published in 1993, we find that the source of horror has shifted. It comes, not from the old Soviet bloc, but from North Africa and the Middle East catalysed by the rise of a massive military power determined to move out of Asia and devastate Europe. In this lurid scenario all will not be lost, however, because a successful counter-attack will be launched from British shores.

One of the *quatrains* which has been relied upon as confirmation of the clap-trap predictions about what is in store for us as the year 2000 approaches is that of **CX, Q72**. This prophecy stands alone in that it is one of very few amongst the total of some 960 *quatrains* and more than 100 *présages* which actually includes a date. The French original describes how in:

> *L'an mil neuf cent nonante neuf sept mois,*
> *Du ciel viendra un grand Roy d'effraieur*
> *Ressusciter le grand Roy d'Angoulmois,*
> *Avant après Mars regner par bonheur.*

According to the English translation of de Fontbrune's work, the *quatrain* reveals that, *in July 1999 a great, terrifying leader will come through the skies to revive [the memory of] the great conqueror of Angoulême. Before and after war will rule luckily.*

As has been mentioned, herein rests a pithy illustration of the child's-play ease with which Nostradamus' cloth can, and has been, cut according to the coat which various authors have had in mind and it is therefore worth examining the *quatrain* in more detail.

In the first place, whether intentionally or otherwise, de Fontbrune has conveniently misquoted the old French by introducing the qualifying word *d'effrayeur* in line 2 which has replaced the original expression *d'effraieur*. This substitution may appear academic to the casual observer but it introduces a wealth of difference to the meaning since *d'effrayeur* describes a leader who is *terrifying* whilst *d'effraieur* offers the qualification that he is concerned with provision of *finance*. The English translator not only describes a terrifying leader rather than a financial backer but compounds the error by automatically equating Mars with war. Yet this draws on astrological lore selectively. Aggressive or brutal traits are only the negative aspect of Mars. In its more positive colours it is associated with love of freedom, strong leadership in crisis, decisiveness, defence of the weak, and sexual drive – hardly the stuff of apocalypse! Furthermore the astral conjunctions of Mars for July 1999 place its attributes firmly amongst the latter qualities.

Apart from the allusion to the warlike character of Mars, key elements also include the mention of the king of the Angoulmois and reference to his arrival from the skies. Angoulmois is generally considered to refer to a clan based around the locality of Angoulême, a town in south-west France. The Angoulmois, it is argued, were once conquered by the Visigoths and their land subsequently invaded by the Mongol-derived Huns under the command of Attila. It has been asserted that Angoulmois provides an anagram of Mongolois or 'Mongols'. The 'coming from the skies', coupled with the reference to Mars, has therefore been interpreted to define an airborne invasion of France from Asia in July 1999.

In historical reality the Visigoths were forced across the Danube by the Huns in 376 CE, first establishing themselves in the Balkans before moving into France and Spain. The Visigoths ruled initially as Roman subjects and then independently but their rule in south-west France was destroyed, not by the Huns who had indeed occupied other parts of Gaul in the late fourth and fifth centuries, but by the Franks in 507 CE.

Nonetheless the *quatrain* has regularly been cited in support of the 1999 doomsday argument and it has been fashionable to treat it as an emphatic prophecy of the 'beginning of the end', the dreadful conclusion of the Piscean Age. In 1995 the Nostradamus-watcher, Francis X. King, asked: 'Who, or what, is the King of Terror?' and asserted confidently: 'Almost certainly an individual who will unleash nuclear war upon our planet or, perhaps, an exceptionally large and destructive fusion bomb . . . at the time of the Olympic Games of 2008 a world leader who will be the head of a sinister necromantic cult and may well be the "King of Terror" will carry out an action of major importance connected with "setting the East aflame".'

Does anybody seriously believe that, in 1998, with the United States in a supreme strategic position, with the Soviet bloc virtually bankrupt, with China adopting increasing levels of pragmatism towards the global community, and with such Middle Eastern leaders as those in command of Iraq and Iran looking nervously over their shoulders in case of back-stabbing from within their own ranks, that this measure of catastrophe is about to herald in the Age of Aquarius?

One of the most astute recent observations on Nostradamus comes from the astrologer and psychologist Liz Greene, who reminds us that it is easy to forget that Nostradamus was very much a man of his time, and used to

REFERENCES TO VOLCANIC ERUPTIONS HAVE BEEN DEDUCED FROM A GOOD MANY OF THE PROPHECIES.

the peculiar images and associations of Renaissance symbolism to describe events and persons within his own national and spiritual sphere. He is speaking not in the language of the twentieth century, but in that of the sixteenth. In truth he was working with a dictionary much smaller than that familiar to the twentieth-century scholar and many of the words needed to describe twentieth-century phenomena had not been invented. Therefore, when he talks of 'fiery missiles coming from the skies', he is not alluding to Stealth bombers or SS20 missiles because he has no perception of them. He is probably referring to the appearance of a comet or a volcanic eruption.

At least one more cautionary note of a general nature should be considered when browsing through the prophecies. A number of authors have tried to interpret the bulk of the *quatrains* according to events taking place in France. Any *quatrain* which hints at revolution or republicanism has at once been taken to mean the political upheaval which took place during the eighteenth century in France. Yet if, as has been claimed, Nostradamus was amongst the greatest visionaries of all time, it is hardly likely that his power of foresight was unable to penetrate beyond the borders of his own country. It is true that many of the *quatrains* refer to towns and cities in France,

Switzerland, Germany or Italy but perhaps only because these reflect the extent of Nostradamus' available dictionary. Very few authors, however, examine the prophecies in the context of events taking place in North America, other parts of Europe, the Indian sub-continent, and even China or Japan. The view of Nostradamus' work should, properly, be global.

In conclusion, to suggest that the main focus of Nostradamus' predictions rests on the second half of the twentieth century is thoroughly facile because those who promote the argument fail to take into account the reality of his life and times. If this 'tunnel-vision' approach is dispensed with it no longer becomes obligatory to interpret all the *quatrains* that describe apocalyptic events in the context of the year 2000. Once the analysis becomes liberated from this restriction, which also demands that Nostradamus jumbled up his *quatrains* using some highly complicated time-code which nobody has been able to decipher, the way is opened to a more reasoned argument. Nostradamus compiled the *quatrains* included within each Century of predictions in a sequence which represents, approximately, an orderly chronological progression based on astrological predictive charts. It is to these that we should, sensibly, be looking.

IT SEEMS REASONABLE TO ASSUME THAT NOSTRADAMUS incorporated a number of 'flags' to the dating of his predictions. Although these lay in his future, many now belong firmly in our history and certain incidents are so precisely detailed that it is difficult not to associate them with specific historical events. So it is to prophecies past, those that appear already to have reached fulfilment, that we should look first.

the PROPHECIES in HISTORY

the assumption must also be that Nostradamus rendered his *quatrains* in an ascending numerical order which equates with the advance of time rather than with some obscure chronological hotchpotch. For this reason it is the *quatrain* numbers rather than the Centuries which are the most essential details and the numbering of predictions will, from here on, reflect this priority by abandoning convention and placing the *quatrain* number before that of the Century.

Certain parameters are still undefined. Are the *quatrains* evenly spaced? How long is the interval between them? If **Q72** (**CX**), that which refers specifically to the year 1999, is correctly dated, the intervals cannot be even throughout each of the completed Centuries. The majority of prognostications are concerned with the 450 years between 1550 and 2000 whilst about 25 per cent cover the 1800 years spanning the period from the beginning of the third millennium onwards. It may be, on the other hand, that the intervals between *quatrain* 1 and *quatrain* 72 are fairly regular even though from the year 2000 onwards the intervals become longer.

Seventy-two *quatrains* divisible into a span of 450

A CONTEMPORARY BROADSHEET RECORDS A METEORITE FALL NEAR OXFORD IN 1628: MISTRESS GREENE, A WITNESS, HAS ONE DUG UP, THOUGH ONE OF THE DIGGERS SWOONS IN TERROR.

years suggests that regular spacing will result in intervals of approximately six years. It would be facile to take this figure as being carved in stone. For sake of argument we can be fairly confident that Nostradamus did not compose *quatrain* 10 in whatever Century whilst saying to himself: 'This prediction must relate to events taking place in 1610, not a year less, not a year more' (1550 + 60 years or 10 x 6). We have to assume a degree of latitude.

The 'flags' or milestones in the dating may sometimes be of a manmade kind, detailing battles, coronations, assassinations and other situations. But many relate to naturally occurring events where Nostradamus describes such circumstances as astronomical conjunctions, appearance of comets, solar and lunar eclipses, occurrence of earthquakes, meteor showers and epidemics of plague.

Astronomical signposts of various kinds are peppered throughout much of the span of the *quatrains*. Their frequency must reinforce the argument that Nostradamus intended us to make use of them although, realistically, only a few include sufficient detail to facilitate dating and several others seem nonsensical to the extent that one

ANTOINE CARON'S PAINTING SHOWS ASTRONOMERS OBSERVING AN ECLIPSE. REFERENCES TO EVENTS SUCH AS THESE ENABLE CERTAIN *QUATRAINS* TO BE DATED IN HISTORY.

gains the impression they are included deliberately to mislead. Amongst the earliest *quatrains* **Q2** (*CVIII*) followed by **Q3** (*CIII*), he inserts details of planetary conjunctions, whilst in **Q6** (*CVI*) he provides information about a comet, and these early inclusions are not uncharacteristic of the *quatrains* which follow.

Mention of conjunctions, however, is by no means

evenly spread. There are about twenty-five of any significance included in the *quatrains* yet almost all occur in the first half of each Century. Nineteen appear in *quatrains* from 1 to 52 whilst only six occur in *quatrains* numbered 53 to 100. This imbalance adds weight to the argument that Nostradamus was working through the *quatrains* in approximately a chronological progression since the necessary equipment to extend conjunctions far ahead of his time would not have been readily available. The astronomical charts known to Nostradamus and his contemporaries, whilst being moderately effective, were comparatively crude devices. They impose an additional limitation in that the information they contain tends to be inaccurate by today's standards.

Modern computer technology, coupled with the development of specialized software, provides the facility to project not only into the distant future but also backwards in time and to calculate with a high degree of accuracy when astronomical conjunctions occurred, certainly those between the mid-sixteenth century and the present day. By way of illustration of the pitfalls in the 'conjunction quatrains', **Q44 (CIX)** includes a piece of astronomical nonsense:

> *Migres, migre de Geneve trestous,*
> *Saturne d'or en fer se changera,*
> *Le contre raypoz exterminera tous,*
> *Avant l'a ruent le ciel signes fera.*

> *Leave, leave Geneva everyone. Saturn will change from gold to iron. Those against raypoz {anagram?} will all be slain. Before the charge the sky will show signs.*

Aside from the vague nature of the prophecy, the astronomy indicates a movement from Leo (gold) to Aries (iron) but this progression cannot occur consecutively.

Nostradamus would have been able to calculate certain other natural phenomena with a fair degree of accuracy, including the appearance of certain periodic comets. Halley's Comet had, for example, been making regular visits to our solar system since as early as 373 BCE and its future predictive occurrence in the night sky was known to Nostradamus from charts of his day. He would also have been able to calculate the periods between solar and lunar eclipses. Conversely he would not, based on mathematical calculations, have been able to predict the occurrence of earthquakes so these would have been wholly a matter for foresight, genuine or otherwise. Yet not infrequently he refers to such events and they serve as a useful test of his prophetic ability.

Occasionally he includes comment about 'fire from

the sky' but this is less helpful. It may refer to meteor shower activity or to volcanic eruption but these events occur too regularly to permit pinpointing of dates. The two active European volcanoes, Etna and Stromboli, are in a more or less constant state of emission, whilst meteor showers occur frequently each time the earth's orbit passes through the track of a comet.

One of the more revealing indicators, not only about Nostradamus' timescales but of whether he genuinely possessed the gift of foresight, may lie in his observations concerning the incidence of bubonic plague because usually he refers to it unambiguously and because we have detailed information on its historical occurrence.

When looking at Nostradamus' predictions and testing them against history, some important limitations must be borne in mind, the first of which concerns fallibility. It would be grossly over-optimistic to assume

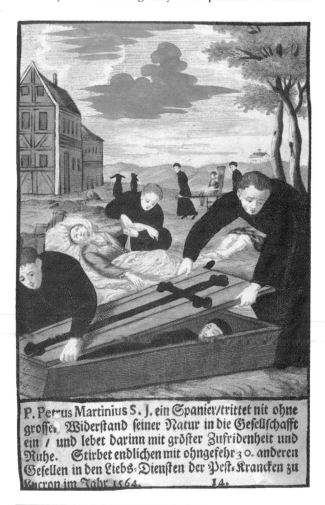

P. Petrus Martinius S. J. ein Spanier/trittet nit ohne grosse Widerstand seiner Natur in die Gesellschafft ein / und lebet darinn mit gröster Zufridenheit und Ruhe. Stirbet endlichen mit ohngefehr 30. anderen Gesellen in den Liebs-Diensten der Pest-Krancken zu Lucron im Jahr 1564. 14.

AS A DOCTOR NOSTRADAMUS TOOK A CLOSE INTEREST IN THE PLAGUE AND THERE ARE NUMEROUS REFERENCES TO 'LA PESTE' IN HIS PREDICTIONS.

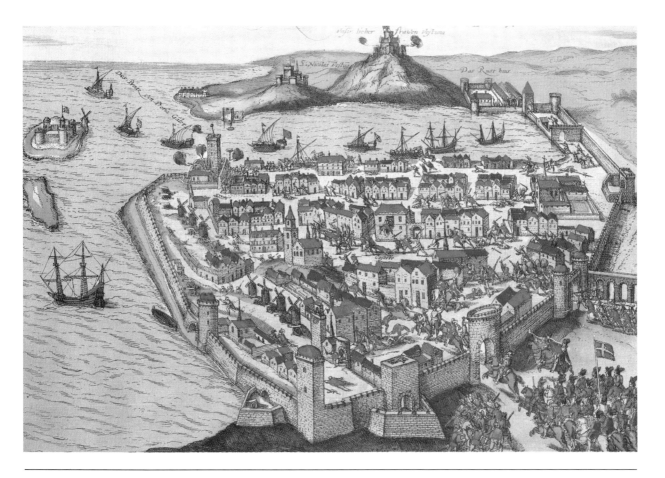

A VIEW OF MARSEILLES IN 1596: THIS SEAPORT WAS MENTIONED SPECIFICALLY BY NOSTRADAMUS BUT MAY HAVE BEEN USED AS A GENERIC TERM.

that Nostradamus 'got it right' every time. There appears to be an astonishing level of accuracy in many of his predictions which suggest that he possessed a genuine gift of foresight but no sensible analyst would claim that they are wholly reliable.

Constant reference is made, throughout the range of *quatrains*, to certain people and places, to the extent that they may have to be regarded as generic terms rather than specifics. The prophecies are, for example, littered with references to 'Henri'. One should not assume that all of these refer to one of the French, English or even German kings of that name but that, as Nostradamus probes deeper into the misty future and further away from the familiarities of the sixteenth century, they may become references to a king or a ruler whose name he does not know. By similar token in the early period covered by the predictions the constant reference to France in war probably does relate to that country, but eventually it becomes a reference to western Europe in the broader sense.

Amongst other reservations we must conclude that

some of the place names need interpreting liberally and with a degree of understanding about knowledge of the world as it existed in the sixteenth century. One cannot expect that Nostradamus' powers of divination necessarily extended to the ability to name New York or Cape Canaveral, not to mention Milton Keynes and Crawley New Town. There is repeated reference to French towns with which he was familiar during his lifetime – Narbonne, Carcassonne, Marseilles and others. Some of the predictions may indeed relate specifically to such named places whilst others may require a degree of 'lateral thinking' to be applied on our part.

Nostradamus also uses the names of a select group of rivers and one should not assume that he necessarily believed it was the Gironde, the Garonne or the Po which always captured attention! Out of convenience he was merely using those names which were familiar to him from his travels in France and Italy to illustrate a point. He may sometimes have been using the names to describe other places with similar characteristics where the predicted events would take place. In other words, he was eventually using proper names to identify *types* because of the limitations imposed by his personal dictionary.

In the pages which follow, certain key elements, the nature of which is not in dispute, have been selected from amongst the hundreds of *quatrains* and the political, military and religious events with which they are contemporary have been checked against predictions in the same or adjacent *quatrains*. The result is often striking.

Shortly after 1555, the year when Nostradamus consigned the inheritance of the prophecies to César, two great comets appeared, one of which was first reported on 27th February 1556. *Q1 (CI)* provides an extraordinary and vividly provocative observation:

Estant assis de nuict secret estude
Seul reposé sur la selle d'aerain;
Flambe exigue sortant de solitude
Fait prosperer qui n'est à croire vain.

Seated alone in the night in secret study; it is placed on the brass tripod; a faint flame comes out of the emptiness and makes successful that which should not be believed in vain.

Here is Nostradamus, closeted in his place of work, with his brass telescope beside him and with the first of his prophecies being committed to paper. Out of the emptiness of the dark night sky emerges the light of a comet, a propitious omen, one of the factors which will 'make successful that which should not be believed in vain'. This, surely, is one of the clearest indications of intent on the part of the author. Nostradamus is telling his son, and anyone else prepared to examine his work intelligently, to *begin at the beginning. Q1 (CI)* is not a prophecy, rather it is an observation on the moment of departure from the present to the future.

The appearance of the comet was a portent, but of what? In other ways the year 1556 held considerable significance. In Italy, it was the year in which Charles V, the Holy Roman Emperor whose reign saw the emergence of the Reformation, abdicated the throne. Disillusioned by internal and foreign wrangles and generally disliked, he

THE ABDICATION OF CHARLES V, THE HOLY ROMAN EMPEROR, APPEARS TO HAVE BEEN FORESEEN BY NOSTRADAMUS.

retired to a Spanish monastery where he died in 1558. *Q2 (CIX)* appears to predict this event well:

Du hault du mont Aventin voix ouye,
Vuydez vuydez de tous les deux costes,
Du sang des rouges sera l'ire acconye
D'Arimin Prato, Columna debotez.

From the heights of the Aventine Hill (Rome) a voice is heard from both sides, Go away, Go away. The red blood will appease the anger. From Rimini and Prato, Columna is expelled.

A startling prediction, almost at the very outset, is that contained in *Q3 (CIII)*. Here we find Nostradamus foretelling an earthquake from the 'depths of Asia', linked to an astronomical conjunction:

46

Mars & Mercure & l'argent joint ensemble,

Vers le midy estreme siccité

Au fond d'Asie on dira terre tremble,

Corinthe, Ephese lors en perplexité.

Mars, Mercury and the Moon in conjunction; towards the south a great drought; from the depths of Asia an earthquake is reported; Corinth and Ephesus are then troubled.

On 24th January 1556, a huge earthquake in northern China, predicted to be felt as far away as the Aegean, resulted in the worst death toll in history when 830,000 people lost their lives.

At an early stage in the *quatrains* one encounters a pithy observation of how Nostradamus' prophecies sometimes need careful evaluation. **Q4 (CVIII)** describes the balance of power changing between France and Italy:

Dedans Monech le coq sera receu,

Le Cardinal de France apparoistra

Par Logarion Romain sera deceu

Foiblesse à l'aigle & force au coq naistra.

The Cockerel will be received in Monaco. The Cardinal of France will appear. He will be deceived by the Roman legation. Weakness to the eagle, and strength will be born in the Cockerel.

Prior to the 1550s Monaco was bound under a treaty with Spain although the Grimaldi dynasty exercised nominal independence. The prediction is that the Cardinal of France will be duped by one of the Italian legates, resulting in power gains by the French cock at the expense of the Roman eagle. On first inspection of the history of the time it may appear that the reverse occurred since the French were ostensibly 'thrown out' of Italy by the Habsburgs in 1559. In reality the Peace of Cateau-Cambrensis (1559) in which this withdrawal was negotiated gave France respite from its long-term rivalry with the Habsburgs and steered Italy into an endless series of debilitating complications in the Balkans and in the Mediterranean. The prediction reveals considerable foresight.

Eclipses feature in the *quatrains* occasionally. The juxtaposition of solar and lunar eclipses is a fairly unusual occurrence, yet such an event is described in **Q4 (CIII)**:

Quand seront proches de defaut des lunaires,

de l'un à l'autre ne distant grandement

Froid, siccité, danger vers les frontières

Mesme où l'oracle a prins commencement.

When the flaw in the moons is close, they will not be very distant from one another. Cold, drought, danger around the frontiers, even where the oracle had its origin.

This is immediately followed by a similar observation in **Q5 (CIII)**:

Pres loing defaut de dux grands luminaires,

Qui surviendra entre l'Avril & Mars:

O quel cherté mais deux grans debonnaires,

Par terre & mer secourrant toutes pars.

Then, after the eclipse of the two great lights which will take place between April and March. Oh what loss! Yet two great influences for good will assist all sides by land and sea.

According to contemporary historians this conjunction of solar and lunar eclipses occurred in 1556. No rain fell from April to August and the following winter was exceptionally harsh. In 1557 England's ongoing polemics with France flared up once more and served to threaten England's borders, the French King Henri II having the advantage of his feet planted firmly in both Calais and Edinburgh.

If we continue to examine the *quatrains* from the start of each Century, they reveal that Nostradamus refers to the plague no less than 10 times in prophecies between *quatrains* 1 and 32 but thereafter mentions it very little. As a doctor treating the disease he had more than usual interest in the subject. He would certainly have been aware of the history of the disease and would have understood that it appeared in epidemic waves.

The first recorded outbreaks of plague can be traced to North Africa in the third century BCE with the initial

A PAINTING FROM THE HOURS OF HENRI II OF FRANCE
ILLUSTRATES THE SAYING 'THE KING TOUCHES, GOD CURES'.

1588 and 1589, with another following in 1629. The Great Plague of Marseilles occurred in 1720 after the disease was imported on a ship from Syria. In the subsequent two-year period 50,000 of Marseilles' inhabitants perished and attempts to arrest the spread of the disease are recorded in an Act of Parliament (of Aix) which exerted the death penalty on anyone found guilty of communication between Marseilles and the rest of Provence.

It would seem that Nostradamus indeed predicted the future course of the plague with considerable accuracy. He may not always have been referring specifically to bubonic plague but to other scourges such as cholera, typhus and to disease in a more generic sense. The way the references are grouped may, however, be revealing of his understanding that the epidemics would occur in waves.

When referring to the plague Nostradamus, the physician, prefers to use the word *peste* and occasionally *pestilence* although it is part of the general record that a localized and particularly virulent variety of plague was known as *le charbon* because of the black pustules it generated. His earliest observation of *le peste* is contained in **Q5 (CVI)**:

> *Si grande famine par vnde pestisère*
> *Par pluye longue le long du polle arctique:*
> *Samarobryn cent lieux de l'hemisphère,*
> *Viuront sans loy exempt de pollitique.*

> *So great a famine by plague-ridden wave, out of long rains in the northern hemisphere. Samarobryn, a hundred leagues from the hemisphere. They will live without law except that of politik.*

Here the physician shrewdly links wet weather with disease sweeping the northern hemisphere and links it to an obscure place or person in the south.

Immediately following this, in **Q6 (CII)** he describes a major epidemic outbreak in coastal cities:

> *Auprès des portes & dedans deux cités,*
> *Seront deux fleaux & oncques n'apperceu un tel*
> *Faim, dedans peste, de fers hors gens boutés,*
> *Crier secours au grande Dieu immortel.*

pandemic breaking out on the Nile estuary in 542 CE. The second major pandemic came out of Asia in the middle of the fourteenth century and lasted throughout the fifteenth century. It was nonetheless active throughout Europe until it waned significantly during the 1660s. The last English outbreak occurred between 1665 and 1666. The most recent of the historical pandemics began in China in 1893 and by 1900 minor outbreaks had been recorded as far away as Europe.

In the south of France, the area most of interest to Nostradamus, there was an epidemic in Provence between

*Near harbours and within two cities, there will occur
two scourges the like of which is unknown: hunger,
plague within, people dispersed by the sword will cry for
help from God immortal.*

It is well documented that plague was particularly prevalent in European seaports, including Marseilles where it was regularly introduced into the population, transmitted through the agency of ship's rats which had carried it from sources including the Middle East where it was more or less endemic.

Outside of plague references, is there any more firm evidence of where *quatrains* 5 and 6 may lie in the timescale? On the basis of six-year intervals the predictions should have reached the 1580s. In **Q6 (CVI)** one discovers reference to a comet:

*Apparoistra vers la Septentrion,
Non loin de Cancer l'estoile chevelue:
Suze, Sienne, Boece, Eretrion,
Mourra de Rome grand, la nuict disperue.*

*It will appear towards the North, the bearded star, not
far from Cancer; Susa, Siena, Boetia, Eritrea, the great
man of Rome will die, the night dispersed.*

A major comet appeared in 1577 on 1 November and this may be corroborated by **Q6 (CVIII)** although the subject matter changes and the timescale is slightly at odds:

*Clarté fulgure à Lyon apparante
Luisant, print Malte subit sera estainte,
Sardon, Mauris traitera decepuante,
Geneve à Londes à coq trahyson sainte.*

*Lightning and brightness appearing at Lyon. Malta is
taken and will be eliminated. Maurice will behave in a
deceitful manner. From Geneva to London treason
towards the cockerel will be feigned.*

The most significant political aspect of this *quatrain* is that Malta had been attacked and overrun by the Turks in 1565. It is also an accurate prediction that during the

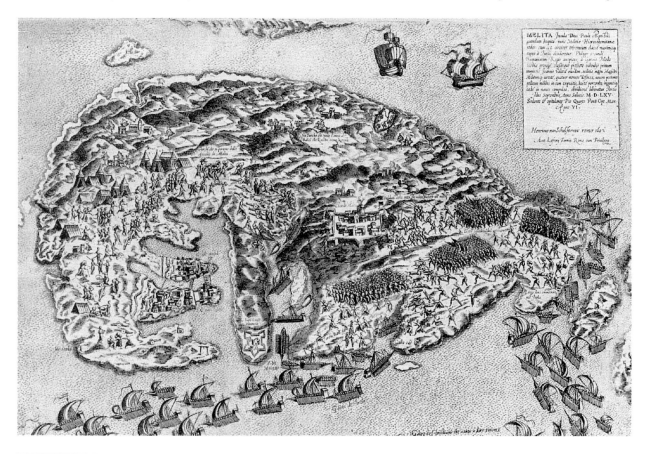

THE SIEGE OF MALTA IN 1565 WAS PREDICTED BY NOSTRADAMUS.

Wars of Religion that took place between 1562 and 1629, France's weakness and preoccupation with internal strife was to the advantage of other nations in Europe, including England under Elizabeth I who established Protestantism there. In the context of loyalty to the Papacy this was undoubtedly a treason in French eyes.

Q7 (CIII) may report the appearance of a comet or asteroids, though in more obscure terms:

> *Les fugitifs, feu du ciel sus les piques.*
> *Conflict prochain des corbeaux s'esbatans*
> *De terre on crie aide secours celiques,*
> *Quand près des murs seront les combatans.*

> *Fire from the sky shall fall on the pikes of the fugitives.*
> *Near to the conflict, crows fight amongst themselves.*
> *From earth the cry for help ascends to the heavens when*
> *the combatants near the walls.*

On the basis of six-year intervals from 1550, *quatrain 7* relates to events taking place in about 1592. During the French Wars of Religion, the years 1589–93 witnessed the grim Siege of Paris. The *quatrain* describes crows, harbingers of death, fighting over the human carrion and cries from those beleaguered within the walls of a city under attack.

Q10 (CI) and *Q11 (CVI)* predict one of the most important political events in the history of France around the turn of the seventeenth century. They involve the famous warnings made by Nostradamus about the fate of the children of Catherine de Medici, his mentor. *Q10 (CI)*:

> *Serpens transmis dans la caige de fer,*
> *Où les enfants septains du Roy sont pris:*
> *Les vieux & pères sortiront bas de l'enfer,*
> *Ains mourir voir de fruict mort & crys.*

AN EARLY-SEVENTEENTH-CENTURY ENGRAVING OF THE SIEGE OF PARIS IN 1590.

CATHERINE DE MEDICI WITH HER SONS CHARLES IX AND HENRI III IMMORTALIZED IN A TAPESTRY.

A shroud is placed in the vault of iron, which holds the seven children of the king. The ancestors and the fathers will arise from the depths of hell, lamenting the dead fruit of their lineage.

In 1610 the mortal remains of one of the offspring, Henri III, the last of the Valois kings of France was exhumed and reinterred in the family tomb at St Denis. Of the seven offspring of Henri II and Catherine de Medici all had, by that time, perished except for Marguerite de Navarre who lived incarcerated in a convent until 1615.

MARGUERITE DE NAVARRE.

Q11 (CVI) is particularly explicit and significant in terms of the overall turn of events:

Des sept rameaux à trois front reduicts,
Les plus asinez seront surprins par mort,
Fraticider les deux seront seduicts,
Les conjurez en dormans seront morts.

The seven branches will be reduced to three, the elder ones will be surprised by death. Two will be attracted towards fratricide, the conspirators will die in their sleep.

By 1575, of the seven siblings, only Henri, François d'Alençon and Marguerite de Navarre were surviving. The heir to the throne, Charles IX, had died in 1574. Henri became Henri III, King of France, but François became embroiled in a series of plots, joining forces with the League of the Holy Court, Europe's senior secret society led by the Ducs de Guise, through whose assistance he aspired to the throne by way of his brother's death. The Leaguers, for their part, were determined to suppress the liberality provoked by the openly homosexual Henri. The principal plotters, the Duc and Cardinal de Guise, were murdered at Blois in 1588 on the orders of Henri who had become perennially embroiled in religious wars between Catholics and Huguenots, and his clash with the Leaguers led to his own assassination in 1589. It was the Bourbon King Henri IV, reigning from 1589 to 1610, who pulled France clear of the morass of religious dissent.

In *Q10 (CVIII)* there is mention of 'fire seen in the sky' which rests fairly well, chronologically, with a comet that became visible in 1618:

Puanteur grands sortira de Lausanne
Qu'on ne saura l'origine du fait,
Lon mettra hors toute la gent loingtaine
Feu veu au ciel, peuple estranger deffait.

A great smell will emanate from Lausanne but its origin will be unknown. People from far away will be put out; fire is seen in the sky, a foreign people is defeated.

No major losses of sovereignty occurred around this time in Europe but between 1610 and 1612, during the

Russo-Polish wars, the Poles occupied the Kremlin. A commemorative tablet in the monastery of Zagorsk near Moscow reads: 'Typhus – Tartars – Poles: Three Plagues'.

By *quatrain* 10, Nostradamus is also making several predictions about the millennium. In **Q10 (CII)** he warns:

> *Avant long temps le tout sera rangé*
> *Nous esperons un siecle bien senestre:*
> *L'estat des masques & des seuls bien changé*
> *Peu trouveront qu'a son rang vueille estre.*

> *Before long all will be arranged. We anticipate a very evil century: the condition of the masked and lonely people will be much altered, few will find that they wish to retain their position.*

Most commentators see this as a premonition of the French Revolution of 1789 in which the lives of the aristocracy, *les masques*, and the celibate clergy, *les seuls*, were turned upside down by the abolition in 1790 of their classes.

A further plague reference occurs in **Q10 (CVI)** which seems also to serve as a colourful portent of the approaching millennium:

> *Un peu de temps les temples des couleurs*
> *De blanc & noir des deux entremeslée:*
> *rouges & jaunes leur embleront les leurs.*
> *Sang, terre, peste, faim, feu, d'eau assollée.*

> *Soon the temples of the colours, black and white will be mingled. Red and yellow will become other emblems. Blood, earth, plague, hunger, fire, crazed by thirst.*

Nostradamus generates colourful imagery of the Four Horsemen of the Apocalypse bringing their individual torments to humankind.

A significant and fairly specific prediction emerges in **Q11 (CIX)**:

> *Le juste a tort à mort lon viendra mettre*
> *Publiquement & due millieu estaint:*
> *Si grande peste en ce lieu viendra naistre*
> *Que le jugeans fouyr feront constraint.*

> *The just man will come to be wrongly put to death, killed publicly and in their midst. So great a plague will be born in this place, that the judges will be obliged to flee.*

The immediate inference here is that the *quatrain* refers to the death of England's Charles I by public execution, followed by the Great Plague of London in 1655 and 1666. This would, unfortunately, put the chronology out of step. There was, however, another 'official murder' in England, less well publicized, but one which took place in 1613, close to the rough date of 1616 calculated for *quatrain* 11. In the words of the historian Godfrey Davies, 'no single event did more to lessen the general reverence

THE EXECUTION OF CHARLES I FROM A CONTEMPORARY BROADSHEET: WAS THIS EVENT PREDICTED BY NOSTRADAMUS?

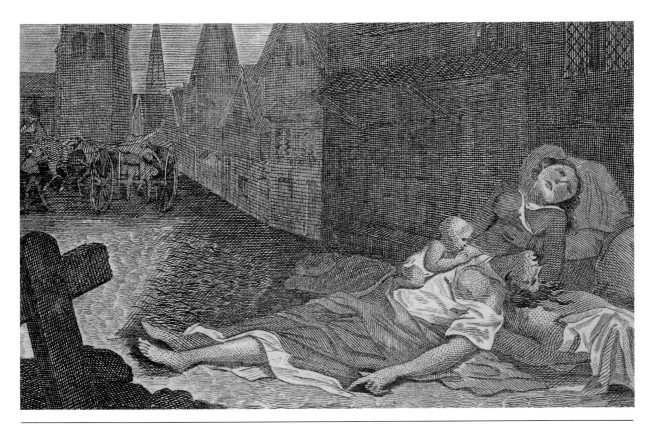

THE GREAT PLAGUE OF LONDON: THE PLAGUE PREDICTED IN *QUATRAIN* 11? BOTH THIS AND THE DEATH OF THE MONARCH ARE CONTENTIOUS INTERPRETATIONS.

with which royalty was regarded in England than this unsavoury episode.' The occasion was the disgraceful poisoning in the Tower of London of Sir Thomas Overbury, carried out on the instructions of King James I to smooth the path of an illicit love match involving the Earl of Rochester and the Countess of Essex. This liaison had been strongly opposed by Overbury, the 'just man'.

At least seven great comets appeared during the seventeenth century. That of 1618 was followed by sightings in 1664, 1665 and 1668. *Q15 (CII)* links the appearance of a comet with warning of the impending death of a king, apparently with reference to an Italian situation:

Un peu devant monarque trucidé
Castor, Pollux en nef, astre crinite
L'erain public par terre & mer vuidé;
Pise, Ast, Ferrare, Turin, terre interdicte.

Shortly before a king meets his end Castor and Pollux in the ship, a bearded star. Public funds expended on land and sea; Pisa, Asti, Ferrara and Turin are barred lands.

SIR THOMAS OVERBURY, A VICTIM OF COURT INTRIGUE AND POSSIBLY THE 'JUST MAN' OF Q11.

Hitherto, no satisfactory explanation has been advanced for this *quatrain* which appears to be forward-looking with a cometary appearance presaging things to come, including the death of another king or, perhaps, the termination of a crown. There is a possibility which may also explain the Castor and Pollux reference. In 1687 the seven-hundred-year-old elective monarchy of Hungary, recently liberated from the Ottomans, was abolished under the despotic designs of the Austrian Habsburg liberators, the ancient right of the Magyar aristocracy was cancelled and, under the Peace of Carlowitz in 1699, Austria and Hungary became conjoined. Not ideal heavenly twins sailing together in the boat, but perhaps something of what Nostradamus foresaw. As to the Italian reference, this is a fairly accurate prediction of the longstanding and shifting divisions which existed in Italy in the seventeenth and eighteenth centuries between the divine autocracy of the Papal States in the 'midriff' of the country and the city republics of which Ferrara was certainly a significant member and which effectively prevented annexation of the Papal States until 1870.

Plague is mentioned in **Q17 (CVIII)**, **Q19 (CII)** and **Q19 (CIII)** followed by **Q21 (CVIII)**. The first of these includes reference to 'three brothers':

> *Les bien aisez subit seront desmis*
> *Par les trois frères le monde mis en trouble,*
> *Cité marine daiseront ennemis,*
> *Faim, feu, sang, peste & de to'maux le double.*

> *The complacent will suddenly be put out, the world placed in trouble by the three brothers. Enemies will capture a coastal city. Hunger, fire, blood, plague; all evils doubled.*

If this *quatrain* takes us forward on the timescale 102 years from 1550, it is remarkably accurate if one accepts that 'three brothers' is a euphemism. The year 1652 saw the commencement of the Three Anglo-Dutch Wars over Dutch freedom of navigation in the Channel and the North Sea. The English did not capture any Dutch ports but they effectively blockaded the coast, causing economic chaos.

After *quatrain* 21 there is a marked dearth of references to the plague and if the *quatrains* proceed in an

'THE DUTCH IN THE MEDWAY' BY J. PEETERS RELATES TO THE ANGLO-DUTCH WARS OVER DISPUTED NAVIGATION RIGHTS.

approximately chronological order, the pattern suggests that Nostradamus predicted accurately that the medieval incidence of the disease would burn itself out.

In contrast, his reference to earthquakes continues and provides fascinating conjecture. One should not assume, however, that the incidents he refers to necessarily relate to Europe. He seems to demonstrate a remarkable ability to predict major seismological disruptions anywhere on the planet. A major earthquake mention is included in *Q20 (CI)*:

Tours, Orléans, Blois, Angiers, Reims & Nantes,
Cités vexées par subit changement:
Par langues estranges seront tendues tentes,
Fleuves, dards Renes, terre & mer tremblement.

Tours, Orléans, Blois, Angers, Reims and Nantes are upset by sudden change. There will be an attack by people of foreign tongues. Rivers, darts at Rennes, earth and sea quake.

There was no significant earthquake in Europe in the late 1600s but in 1692 there took place a massive quake in the Caribbean area which obliterated Port Royal in Jamaica. The period also coincides with the Nine Years War, from 1689 to 1697. In 1686 the League of Augsberg was initiated by William of Orange in order to arrest further French ambitions for expansion. Louis XIV defied the League and a series of sieges and naval battles resulted when Louis was forced to abandon most of his acquisitions. The effect would certainly have been felt throughout French towns and cities.

There is a useful astronomical conjunction described in *Q25 (CV)*:

Le prince Arabe Mars, Sol, Venus, Lyon,
Regne d'Eglise par mer succombera:
Devers la Perse bien près d'un million,
Bisance, Egypte, ver. serp. invadera.

The Arab prince, Mars, Sun, Venus, Leo, the rule of the Church will succumb by the sea. Towards Persia nearly a million will invade Byzantium (Constantinople) and Egypt.

THE EARTHQUAKE THAT DESTROYED PORT ROYAL IN JAMAICA IN 1692 APPEARS TO HAVE BEEN FORESEEN IN THE *QUATRAINS*.

The *quatrain* takes the predictive sequence to about 1700 and this particular conjunction occurred in August 1699 and July 1701.

This is a curious prediction which appears to make little sense on first reading and it is probably one of those *quatrains* that is correct in spirit though not in detail. The year 1699 saw the Peace of Carlowitz which marked a great turning point in the fortunes of the Ottoman Empire, which included Egypt, captured in 1517. From 1684 onwards the Turks were being pushed back down the Danube Valley until, in 1699, Leopold I of Habsburg Hungary halted the advance and offered settlement terms. These included the restoration of Transylvania and Hungary to the Habsburgs, Kamanets Podolskiy to Poland, Morea to Venice and Azov in the Crimea to Russia. The concessions did not destroy the Turkish Empire, nor did they put a million fighting men into Constantinople, but they effectively reduced the power of Constantinople to the point where the Turkish Empire was no longer a threat to Europe and, in the longer term, the European provinces of the Ottomans were squeezed disastrously between the Habsburgs and the Russians.

A new cluster of plague outbreaks is mentioned in **Q30 (CIV)** and **Q32 (CII)** and, on the basis of six-year intervals between predictions, *quatrain 30* should more or less coincide with the time in about 1732 when Nostradamus anticipated that the prelude to the millennium would open. The notion that, in some way, he foresaw the millennium starting in the year 2000 cannot be taken seriously unless one is of the opinion that he was completely out of step with the other prophets of his time. There is little to support this view and, on the contrary, Nostradamus has offered a specific date when he believes the millennium countdown will begin. He predicted, in the interim period of 177 years, 3 months and 11 days, a time of plague, long famines, wars, and floods by which he appears to refer to uprisings of a political rather than watery nature. Curiously, however, he did not envisage the commencement of the millennium machinery being marked by a shift into peace and tranquillity. This incidentally also holds against the case of those who claim that the millennium date is predicted to occur around the year 2000 since nowhere, apparently, in the entire span of the *quatrains* does the strife come to an end! Even in the final *quatrain* of Century X he has great invasion forces on the move.

Q32 (CII) refers to an outbreak of plague occurring in Balennes or Trebula Balliensis near Capua in southern Italy but it also makes reference to the Balkans:

Laict, sang, grenouilles escoudre en Dalmatie,
Conflict donné, peste près de Balennes
Cry sera grand par toute Esclauonie,
Lors naistra monstre près & dedans Ravenne.

Milk, blood, frogs will be prepared in Dalmatia,
battle waged and plague near Balennes. The cry will
be great throughout Slavonia, then a monster will be
born near Ravenna.

History reveals that an outbreak of bubonic plague occurred in the Balkans between 1770 and 1772 and it was spasmodically active in southern Italy. Equally interesting is the reference to the 'monster born near Ravenna'. The nearest major town on the eastern Italian seaboard is Rimini, the birthplace of Pope Clement XIV who reigned from 1769–74. In 1772 Charles III of Spain dispatched an aggressive ambassador to the Holy See in the form of one José Monino, whose task it was to harry the Pope into suppression of the Jesuits. In the words of Pius XII: 'Under the pressure of the unjust and envious secular forces of the times in a sea of dark forebodings, a Father's hand sacrificed it (the Society of Jesus) for the tranquillity of the bark of Peter.' Clement XIV acquiesced and the Catholic world was thrown into chaos.

Immediately prior to the latter *quatrain* one finds **Q31 (CIX)**. Although the geographical location of the event which it describes is vague, the timing seems remarkably accurate and it must be said that the incident exerted a profound influence on European thought in the eighteenth century. The predictive reference is also incontrovertible, that of the great earthquake which struck Lisbon on All Saints' Day, 1 November 1755 with a magnitude of 8.6, killing 60,000 people:

Le tremblement de terre à Mortara,
Cassiche saint George à demy persondrez
Paix assoupie, la guerre esueillera
Dans temple à Pasques abysmes ensondrez.

The shaking of the earth at Mortara, the tin island of
St George, half sunk. Drowsy with peace, war will
break out at Easter, in the temple abysses will open.

No such place as Mortara exists in Portugal although inland, east-north-east of Lisbon, lies the town of Mora and the reference is possibly inaccurate. The quake was the first to be scientifically recorded. It generated huge waves, drowning thousands and causing widespread damage and there is evidence that it was felt much further afield, causing flooding and loss of life. By way of illustration it is noted that 10,000 died in Morocco and the effects were undoubtedly felt on the shores of Britain, St George's isles, where shock waves were experienced as

POPE CLEMENT XIV WAS COERCED INTO SUPPRESSING THE JESUITS, CAUSING DISRUPTION THROUGHOUT THE CATHOLIC WORLD.

Où tout bon est tout bien Soleil & Lune
East abondant sa ruine s'approche:
Du ciel s'advance vaner la fortune,
En mesme estat que la Septiesme roche.

Where all is good and all is well, in the sun and moon
great ruin approaches. It comes from the sky as you boast
your fortunes, in the same state as the seventh rock.

It should be remembered that comets were regarded as portents of great events and in 1769, only a few years before the dreadful happenings already described, the great Messier comet was seen, remaining visible for 94 days. The sequence of events is remarkable considering that Nostradamus believed the countdown to the new millennium would begin in about the fourth decade of the eighteenth century and it seems clear that his mention of the 'seventh rock' is a biblical reference which also has links with comets and earthquakes. In its first verse Revelation 8 describes the opening of the seventh seal which, in biblical terms, was a tablet of stone. A few verses on in the same chapter the narrator describes how in his vision 'the angel took the censer, and filled it with fire of the altar, and cast it into the earth: and there were voices, and thunderings, and lightnings, and an earthquake … and there fell a great star from heaven, burning as it were a lamp.'

In **Q34 (CIII)** Nostradamus predicts a solar eclipse and links this with the appearance of some frightful individual or circumstance:

Quand le deffaut du Soleil lors sera,
Sur le plain jour le monstre sera veu:
Tout autrement on l'interpretera,
Cherté n'a garde nul n'y aura pourveu.

When the eclipse of the sun take place in broad daylight,
the monster will appear. It will be interpreted in
various ways. It will be not be concerned for money nor
for other matters.

far north as Scotland. The reference to abysses opening in the temple was perhaps also prophetic since the quake undermined the most entrenched hopes of enlightenment, shaking belief in a benign, rational God to the very core since it brought ruin to the just and the unjust in equal measure and was allied in the minds of the populace with the plague as evidence of divine retribution.

Nostradamus was also chillingly close to being accurate in his reference to a new war, since the Seven Years War involving Prussia, Britain and Hanover in bloody conflict with Saxony, Austria, France, Sweden and Russia erupted a year later in 1756 with the devastating attack on Saxony by Frederick the Great of Prussia. The conflict opened after eight years of comparative tranquillity in a Europe constantly racked by warfare during the seventeenth and eighteenth centuries.

Linking these events may be a cometary appearance mentioned in **Q32 (CV)**:

A partial eclipse of the sun took place in 1765 which again suggests that the predictions around *quatrain* numbers 30 to 35, irrespective of the Century volume in which they are found, relate to happenings in the middle decades of the eighteenth century. The reference to the monster which cares not for money or other possessions is typically obtuse but it should be remembered that such occurrences as solar eclipses, earthquakes and comets heralded events shortly to come about. Just four years later, in 1769 in Ajaccio, Corsica, the birth was announced of an infant named Napoleon Bonaparte.

It may be assumed, on the yardstick of plague outbreaks, appearances of comets and incidence of earthquakes, that by roughly *quatrain 35* we have reached the third quarter of the eighteenth century, some 220 years from the date of the letter to César.

This calculation is fascinating if the 1999 date included in *Q72 (CX)* is to be taken as read. By projecting from the 1770s to the 1990s the time period extends by roughly another 220 years but it also includes about an equal number of *quatrains* to that which was taken up by the earlier time span. The calculation also suggests that the quatrain numbers are separated, on average, by five or six years although this cannot be taken as a hard and fast rule.

Sometimes the intervals may be longer, sometimes shorter.

Much has been made of the celebrated *quatrain Q35 (CI)* which it is claimed describes the death of Henri II of France after a lance, carried by a young captain of his Scottish guard, pierced his helmet in a joust in 1559:

> *Le lyon jeune le vieux surmontera,*
> *En champ bellique par singulier duelle:*
> *Dans caige d'or les yeux luy crevera,*
> *Deux classes une, puis mourir mort cruelle.*

> *The young lion will vanquish the elder one, in single combat on the battlefield; he will pierce the eyes in their golden cage; two wounds in one, thence to meet a cruel death.*

This explanation would, however, demolish the argument of the time sequence since *quatrain 35* requires the death to have taken place in or around 1760. September 1759 saw the decisive Battle of Quebec in the Seven Years War

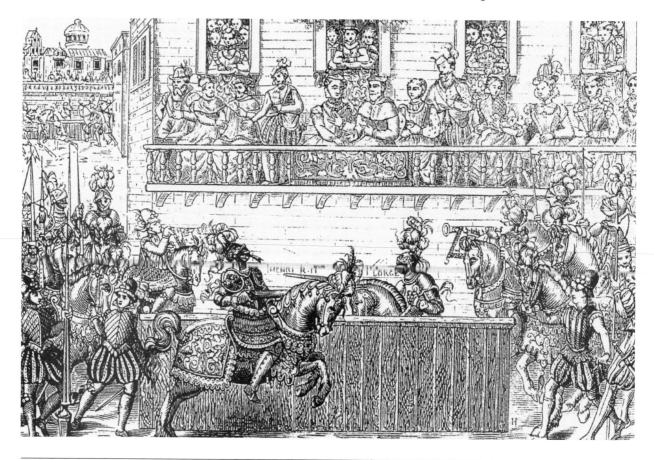

BOTH THE OPENING AND CLOSE OF HENRI II'S REIGN WERE MARKED BY PERSONAL COMBAT. THIS ENGRAVING SHOWS
THE KING'S DEATH IN A TOURNAMENT IN 1559. WAS THIS THE SUBJECT OF *QUATRAIN 35*?

wound. It is as if he were the only important figure in history since 1550 to be killed on the battlefield by a younger adversary.

The next comet appearance which Nostradamus considers to be significant is described in **Q41 (CII)** and again in **Q43 (CII)** which, on the yardstick above, takes us to the start of the second decade of the nineteenth century. On 11th April 1811 the 'Great Comet' was reported. It remained visible in the night sky for an unprecedented 260 days. The following year Napoleon made the catastrophic error of judgement that launched his ill-fated campaign against Russia. At the end of June his Grand Army of some 450,000 men crossed the river Niemen and advanced on Moscow. Six months later he was in full retreat through a landscape devastated by 'scorched earth'. He lost some 250,000 killed and 100,000 taken prisoner. The defeat marked the beginning of the end of the Napoleonic empire.

Q41 (CII) is an extraordinary prophecy. It follows on, indirectly, from **Q39 (CII)** which details, in line 2: *Germains, Gaulois, Haspaignols pour le fort ...* 'Germans, French and Spanish [will be] for the strong one'.

MORE PLAUSIBLY, THE FAMOUS *QUATRAIN* MAY HAVE REFERRED TO THE DEATH OF GENERAL WOLFE IN THE BATTLE OF QUEBEC.

La grande estoille par sept jours bruslera
Nuée fera deux soleils apparoir:
Le gros mastin toute nuict hurlera,
Quand grand pontife changera de terroir.

The great star will burn for seven days and cloud {the comet beard} will make it seem as two suns. The large hound will howl all night when the great pontiff will change his abode.

between the English and French in North America. On the Plains of Abraham near the city both commanders, Major-General James Wolfe and Major-General Marquis Louis-Joseph de Montcalm, were slain. A youthful musketeer, the 'young lion' of England, shot de Montcalm twice, and the Major-General died from his injuries, thus his 'eyes were blinded' and the French army was defeated.

This illustration exposes the errant nonsense of throwing whimsical interpretations at *quatrains* without first possessing a timescale against which they may be set. Yet many authors have slavishly agreed that **Q35 (CI)** must refer to the death of Henri II, largely on the strength of claims that he wore a gilt helmet and suffered a head

In the late eighteenth century the poor treatment of Popes caused considerable upset and controversy, particularly in traditionally Catholic countries like France. In a disgraceful episode Pius VII was arrested by the French authorities in 1809 and imprisoned for nearly five years for excommunicating 'robbers of Peter's patrimony' whose numbers included Napoleon, the 'large hound'. In 1804 he had humiliated the Papacy by persuading the Pope to come to Paris as superintendent of his coronation as Emperor but then placing the crown, in the final moment, upon his own head.

POPE PIUS VII WHO, IN 1804, WAS LURED TO PARIS BY NAPOLEON ONLY TO BE HUMILIATED WHEN THE LATTER TOOK THE EMPEROR'S CROWN FOR HIMSELF.

Q43 (CII) is no less accurate in its prediction:

Durant l'estoille chevelue apparente
Les trois grans princes seront faits ennemis:
Frappés du ciel paix terre tremulente,
Pau, Timbre undans, serpent sus le bort mis.

During the appearance of the bearded star, the three great
princes will be made enemies: the fragile peace on earth
will be struck from the skies, the Po, the Tiber, winding,
a serpent puts ashore.

This *quatrain* seems slightly out of sequence although there was, in fact, an earlier appearance of the Great Comet in 1807. That 'the three great princes will be made enemies' more or less accurately predicts the fall of the so-called Third Coalition forged by the English war leader, Pitt, in 1805 between Great Britain, Austria

and Russia. It was smashed by Napoleon after the rout of the Austrian army at Austerlitz and the Russian forces at Friedland. Subsequently the emperors of France and Russia met on a raft in the river Niemen and signed the Treaty of Tilsit. The reference to the rivers Po and Tiber relates to the annexation of Italy by Napoleon in 1805.

The next major comet described by Nostradamus is included in the lines of **Q46 (CI)**:

Tout auprès d'Aux, de Lestore & Mirande,
Grand feu du ciel en trois nuicts tumbera:
Cause adviendra bien strupende & mirande
Bien peu après la terre tremblera.

Near Aux, Lectoure and Mirande, a great fire will fall from the sky for three nights. The cause will seem both baffling and miraculous. Shortly thereafter the earth will tremble.

No major earthquake is recorded during this period but one of the brightest recorded comets, with a magnitude in excess of three (easily detected with the naked eye), appeared in 1843 as the Great March Comet. Minor earth tremors, it has to be said, tended to go unrecorded.

A further conjunction which includes useful detail from the viewpoint of chronology is that contained in **Q48 (CII)**:

La grande copie qui passera les monts,
Saturne en l'Arq tournant du Poisson Mars:
Venins cachés soubz testes de saulmons,
Leur chef pendu à fil de pole-mars.

SEVERAL QUATRAINS APPEAR TO RELATE TO NAPOLEON'S EMPIRE-BUILDING CAMPAIGN. IN 1805 AT AUSTERLITZ THIS WAS STILL IN THE ASCENDANT.

This *quatrain* is full of obscure euphemisms and seems to use the Latin *copia* (forces) to describe an army. 'The great army will traverse the mountains, Saturn in Sagittarius turning from Mars in Pisces. Poison is hidden under the heads of salmon, their leader hung by a cord of war.'

In terms of the timescale *quatrain* 48 is required to reflect events close to 1838. The conjunction occurred between January and March 1840. One obvious geographical location in which to search for meanings is the mountainous north-west frontier region of India where the British Army was engaged. In 1839, on the orders of Lord Auckland, the first to be titled 'Governor-General of India', the British army marched from the north-west provinces over the mountains into Afghanistan by way of the Bolan Pass to counter the imperial expansionist plans of Russia. The 'grand force', under the command of Sir William Hay Macnaughten, entered Kandahar in April 1839 and some leaders of the opposing forces were hung. The British army of occupation remained in Afghanistan until the autumn of 1841. 'Poison under the heads of salmon' defies precise interpretation, although Erika Cheetham points out that, in the language of Old Provence, *saulmon* is a euphemism for a donkey and the British army relied greatly on mules to carry its supplies, including armaments, across mountainous routes on the north-west frontier.

During this time there are other occasional and isolated mentions of plague, although sometimes one has to be wary of the sense in which the term is used. In **Q49** (**CV**) the term *peste* describes disease though in a less than obvious fashion:

> *Nul de l'Espaigne mais de l'antique France*
> *Ne fera esleu pour le tremblant nacelle,*
> *A l'ennemy fera faicte fiance,*
> *Qui dans son regne sera peste cruelle.*

> *Not from Spain but from old France will he be elected for the trembling vessel. He will make a pact with the enemy who will be a cruel plague in his reign.*

On the basis of an average interval of six years, *quatrain* 49 should take us towards the close of the 1850s. In 1852

Louis Napoleon made himself Emperor of France, Napoleon III, through a *coup d'état* and reverted to the old style of government modelled on that of his more famous uncle, Bonaparte, having overthrown the republican parliamentary regime with the clear intention of reviving the 'old France' of Napoleon I. He was indeed destined to make a strategic pact with an old enemy of France. In March 1854, having been engaging in diplomatic manoeuvres since at least 1852, France joined forces with Britain to fight the Crimean War against Russia over the vexed 'Eastern question'. This involved disputes over administration of shrines in the Holy Land and the protection of Orthodox Christians in Turkey, but essentially it was about the balance of power in Eastern Europe. The consequence was indeed a cruel plague. The ineptitude of military leadership during the war led to enormous losses amongst the allies, largely through cholera and typhus which became rampant in the frozen camps during the siege of Sebastopol.

NAPOLEON III MADE A PACT WITH BRITAIN OVER THE CRIMEAN WAR: THIS COULD BE THE PACT REFERRED TO BY NOSTRADAMUS.

The next environmental catastrophe of an unmistakable nature to which Nostradamus makes clear reference, and which can be partly validated from historical records, is an earthquake at sea described in **Q52 (CII)**:

Dans plusieurs nuits la terre tremblera:
Sur le printemps deux effors suite:
Corinthe, Ephese aux deux mers nagera,
Guerre s'esmeut par deux vaillans de luite.

For several nights the earth will shake; in the spring two
great upheavals one after the other. Corinth and Ephesus
will bathe in two seas. War will begin between two
valiant warriors.

A major earthquake which took the lives of 27,000 people occurred 93 miles off the coast of the Japanese island of Honshu on 15th June 1896. It was preceded by a major quake off the coast of Peru in August 1868. The implication seems similar to that found in **Q3 (CIII)** that major seismological disturbances in Asia and beyond will be felt in the cities of the eastern Mediterranean. Assuming, from the timescale already calculated, that *quatrain* 52 takes us to the period around the 1870s, both of these natural events may reasonably qualify to validate the dating, with the Peru quake coming closer in terms of the chronology.

Plague is described in **Q55 (CIX)** and also in **Q63 (CV)** but again the sense is accountably different and in both Nostradamus employs other words as if to caution us that the subject is dissimilar. In the former *quatrain* he refers to 'la pestilence' and in the latter to 'plagues'. On the basis of timescale, **Q55 (CIX)** should refer to hostilities taking place in about the 1880s:

L'horrible guerre qu'en l'occident s'apreste
L'an ensuivant viendra la pestilence,
Si fort horrible que jeune, vieux, ne beste,
Sang, feu, Mercure, Mars, Jupiter en France.

The frightful war which is prepared in the west, the next
year will bring pestilence so awful that neither young,
nor old, nor beast will survive the blood, fire, Mercury,
Mars, Jupiter in France.

A degree of anticipation seems inherent here. Perhaps the key word, in line 1, is 'prepared' since no major hostility broke out at the onset of the 1880s. But preparations for hostility were afoot and to understand the context it is necessary to consider the political situation existing in Europe. In 1870 six great powers prevailed – France, Germany, Italy, Russia, Austro-Hungary and the Ottoman Empire. Frontiers seemed not to be in dispute but the Achilles heel lay with the crumbling Ottoman Empire and this weakness in central and eastern Europe complicated relations between the other powers. In 1878 a settlement was attempted with the Congress of Berlin but it was destined to fail and because of this and feuds over colonial possessions, the powers separated into two rival alliances which, in 1914, were drawn into the First World War. This was indeed a conflict in which 'pestilence so awful' reigned. The end of hostilities also coincided with an influenza epidemic in which millions died.

THE HORRIFIC SLAUGHTER OF THE FIRST WORLD WAR MAY HAVE BEEN THE PESTILENCE PREDICTED IN QUATRAIN 55.

Q63 (CV) should take the period to the early 1930s and, once more, the insight of Nostradamus proves fascinating. Here he refers to a situation developing in Italy:

De vaine emprise l'honneur indue plaincte,
Galiotz errans par latins froit faim, vagues:
Non loing du Timbre de sang la terre taincte.
Et sur humains seront diverses plagues.

From vain enterprise, honour and undue complaint,
boats wander amongst the Latins, cold, hungry,
waves: not far from the Tiber, the land is tainted
with blood and various plagues fall upon mankind.

By 1928 democracy had effectively collapsed in Italy and been replaced by authoritarian government. One of the most extreme of these systems was the Fascist Party established by Mussolini and his Blackshirts

THE PREDICTION OF UNREST IN ITALY MATCHES THAT COUNTRY'S SLIDE INTO HOSTILITIES UNDER THE LEADERSHIP OF MUSSOLINI.

which, in 1929, instituted a formal agreement with the Papacy. It was Mussolini who would lead Italy into conflict and ultimate defeat in the Second World War, whilst the Papacy took an undeniably partisan stance beside him. The Papacy has, not infrequently, been described by the euphemism of a vessel. The imagery of its clerics as 'boats' wandering amongst the Italian people, whose land would shortly be tainted with blood and plagues, and rubbing shoulders with the 'vain enterprise and undue complaint' of the Fascists is surprisingly colourful.

If this theory of Nostradamus' dating is correct and the *quatrains*, irrespective of the Century in which they are contained, are spaced at more or less six-year intervals, the 1950s, which mark the end of a four-hundred-year period, will be predicted around *quatrain* 66. It is fortunate, therefore, that one such *quatrain*, **Q66** (**CVI**), includes a prediction which cannot be misconstrued and which can also be validated, the occurrence of an earthquake:

Au fondement de la nouvelle secte,
Seront les oz du grande Romain trouvés,
Sepulchre en marbre apparoistra couverte,
Terre trembler en Avril, mal ensouetz.

At the foundation of a new sect, the bones of a great
Roman shall be found. A marble tomb will be uncovered.
The earth will quake in April, badly buried.

The earthquake did not occur in April of 1950 but in August, and not in Italy but in Assam, India. Yet it was the most massively destructive quake of the decade, measuring 8.4 on the Richter scale, and it claimed the lives of 30,000 people. Three years later, in 1953, one of the most notorious quasi-religious sects of all time was established by an American science fiction writer, Ron Lafayette Hubbard. It achieved worldwide publicity as the Church of Scientology. What then of the remarkable archaeological discovery? Nostradamus made very few references to archaeological discovery yet so significant was this event that he reiterated the prediction in a slightly different context in a contemporary *quatrain* from another Century, **Q66** (**CV**):

Soubs les antiques edifices vestaulx,
Non esloignes d'aqueduct ruiné
De Sol & Lune sont les luisans metaulx,
Ardante lampe Traian d'or buriné.

Under the ancient edifices of the vestals, not far from the
ruin of the aqueduct. There will be glittering metals of
Sun and Moon, the carved lamp of Trajan burning.

Ignore the precise details of this *quatrain* because Nostradamus did not always get things absolutely correct. The importance lies in his accurate prediction of a great archaeological discovery at the turn of the 1950s, one of the most celebrated treasure troves of all time. It was between 1947 and the early 1950s that the Dead Sea Scrolls were unearthed at Q'umran. It is believed that the Scrolls were hidden sometime after the Jewish Revolt of 70 CE in consequence of the reconquest of their lands. Although Trajan ruled as Roman Emperor from

THE DISCOVERY OF THE DEAD SEA SCROLLS IN CAVES AT Q'UMRAN WAS ONE OF THE MOST SIGNIFICANT FINDS THIS CENTURY, AND MAY HAVE BEEN IN NOSTRADAMUS' MIND WHEN HE FORESAW SUCH AN EVENT.

MARTIN LUTHER WAS ONE OF MANY PROTESTANTS WHO BELIEVED THAT THE APOCALYPTIC VISION OF REVELATION ALLUDED TO THE CORRUPTION OF THE PAPACY.

98–117 CE, he is known to have been in Judea as a *legatus* as early as 69 CE, performing a key role in the military action against the Jewish communities. He was responsible for erecting a milestone honouring the Emperor Vespasian which was placed in the Jezreel valley in northern Israel and dated to the second half of 69 CE.

Thus far we have examined no more than a tiny fraction of the seven hundred or so *quatrains* spanning the period from Nostradamus' death to the mid-1950s but we have looked closely at those prophecies which seem to be linked to events that are described unambiguously and that can be safely dated in history.

The next chapter examines the predictions which, on the basis of the timescale proposed, cover the latter half of the twentieth century. This is the particular span of time during which many authors promoting popular 'millennium fever' argue that Nostradamus pitched his prophecies of Armageddon and the Second Coming.

In reality most of those who had come to prominence as prophets in the fifteenth and sixteenth centuries believed that the millennium had already begun and the Second Coming was imminent. This was not an especially new conviction. Messianic prophecies of similar nature, inherited from the ancient world, had periodically come to the surface throughout the Middle Ages coupled with a firm belief that the representatives of the antichrist were abroad and must be vanquished in order to avert the apocalypse. It was not until the seventeenth century that opinion began to shift towards the possibility that the millennium was still to come and was some way off.

From the viewpoint of the sixteenth-century Christian reformers, for whom the Church of Rome had become an anathema, the words of Revelation describing the destruction of Babylon came to hold particular significance. They envisaged Babylon and its downfall as being a clear allusion to Rome and the Papacy, the days of which, in the consideration of many Protestants, were numbered. Martin Luther was notable in his views. After personal revelations of a divine nature, and several visits to Rome, he became convinced that the Papacy was irrevocably corrupt and must fall. Typically, in 1520, he wrote a treatise titled *On the Babylonian Captivity of the Church of God* which promptly attracted a papal bull heavy with condemnation. This he burned publicly in an act of heresy for which he was subsequently excommunicated.

Nostradamus no doubt had mixed sentiments about the exact identity of the antichrist. His cultural make-up included an uneasy mix of Semitism and Roman Catholicism and, most probably, he envisaged the first horseman of the apocalypse to be he who rode upon the red horse, the bringer of the terrible disease whose victims confronted him daily in his work as a plague doctor. It is hard to imagine that he did not share the opinion that the Kingdom of God was at hand and that the dramatic events due to precede it were already taking place. Certainly he would not have been alone in this conviction. In 1589 the English courtier Anthony Marten made the fairly typical observation that there was at large 'a great number of prophets that God doth daily send to admonish all people of the latter day, and to give them warning to be in readiness'.

If the context in which Nostradamus lived is taken properly into account, the arguments that the *quatrains* describing apocalyptic events refer more or less exclusively to the late twentieth century become extremely tenuous. The focus shifts most plausibly to the seventeenth century, the build-up to the millennium predicted to begin in the year 1732. In theory, therefore, *quatrains* which overtly prophesy acts of mass destruction are more likely, though not necessarily, to be targeted on events taking place between the 1580s and the early decades of the 1700s.

Yet this peak of destruction does not notably materialize in the prophecies. Nor, if the millennium was in Nostradamus' sights, did he envisage it as the bringer of peace irrespective of which period in time he predicts it to occur. If it was destined to come during the eighteenth century he certainly gives little indication that he believed it would catapult the world into a period of golden tranquillity.

In many respects his seeming obsession with strife turns out to have been remarkably accurate. If one examines the history of Europe between the sixteenth and nineteenth centuries it reveals an unending catalogue of wars, including the three Great Northern Wars, the Dutch Wars, the Wars of Polish and Austrian Succession, the Seven Years War and the Ottoman Wars, to name only the more serious conflicts.

If we are correct in assuming that Nostradamus gave his attentions evenly to the four hundred years which extended into his future, he was being remarkably generous. He might well have followed traits and impulses with which one can readily sympathize, whereby he was considerably more interested in predicting events destined to take place in his own near future rather than those belonging to some misty and unfamiliar world that lay centuries ahead. Yet it seems that he gave as much attention to the decades at the beginning of the twentieth century as he did to those which would immediately follow his death.

None of this even-handedness is to suggest that Nostradamus either ignored or belittled the close of the second millennium in his predictions, only that he did not focus his attentions on the period specifically, as some would assiduously claim, nor did he single it out to mark the advent of doom!

IT SEEMS ALTOGETHER FACILE TO TAKE *Nostradamus' carefully crafted Centuries and to lump quatrains together at random by applying them on a whimsical 'come hither' basis to events in history. There is an easy and short-sighted game to be played in extracting prophecies which refer, let us say, to the public executions of monarchs and laying them all beneath the scaffold of England's Charles I, or those indicating marital tragedies and linking them with the divorce and death of Diana, Princess of Wales.*

NOSTRADAMUS *in* OUR TIME

i t is an inadequate excuse, one without any discernible foundation in either the text of the *Centuries* or contemporary correspondence, to claim that Nostradamus muddled up the arrangement of his prophetic labours in order to make them unintelligible to any but some ethereal occult circle, including his son. This form of impoverished solution to the enigma of his work also does a profound disservice to the intellect of Nostradamus and his abilities as a seer. This next chapter reveals, to a far greater extent than we have already seen, Nostradamus' intention to provide a sensible chronological progression for his *quatrains*, arranging them in such a way that the *quatrain* numbers rest in parallel like the rungs of ladders placed side by side.

There is also an over-simplification in assuming that Nostradamus was wholly preoccupied with death and destruction. It is true that many of his *quatrains* relate to military and strategic matters but, as will be seen, he has predicted, with considerable accuracy, other events of less violent or apocalyptic aspect, including such far-ranging topics as social scandals amongst royal circles and man's first landing on the moon.

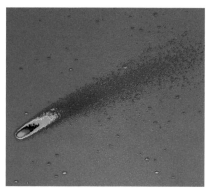

LIKE MANY BEFORE HIM, NOSTRADAMUS REGARDED COMETS AS PORTENTS OF SIGNIFICANT EVENTS.

On the basis that *quatrain* numbers around the middle 60s relate to the mid-twentieth century and that those in the early 70s detail happenings around the year 2000 no more than about 60 *quatrains* apply to our present decades. This is because two of the Centuries are so truncated that, on the basis of this timescale, their *quatrain* numbers do not reach the desired time period and others are incomplete.

Are we safe, however, to accept **Q72** (**CX**), the reference to 1999, as an accurate indicator of the dating scale? Unfortunately a degree of ambiguity exists over Nostradamus' inclusion of year dates and it is demonstrated succinctly in another *quatrain* including specifics, **Q2** (**CVI**):

En l'an cinq cens octante plus & moins,
On attendra le siecle bien estrange:
En l'an sept cens, & trois cieux en tesmoings.
Que plusieurs regnes un à cinq feront change.

In the year five hundred and eighty more or less, one will be in store for a very strange century. In the year seven hundred and three, the skies will be witness that several kingdoms, one to five, will make a change.

This *quatrain* offers two precise year dates though says little else of interest apart from the prophecy that several states will undergo changes. Interest should rest on the manner in which the years are described because Nostradamus chose to omit the 'one thousand' prefix. Clearly he was not referring to 580 or 703 CE since these dates are in the past. The suggestion has been made by Erika Cheetham that Nostradamus nearly always left out the thousand for reasons of scanning, yet this is a grossly inaccurate observation and, in fact, in almost all other *quatrains* he did not omit the thousand figure.

In *Q54 (CVI)*, for example, the fourth line reads: *L'an mil six cens & sept, de Liturgie*, 'In the year sixteen hundred and seven by the Liturgy'. In *Q49 (CI)* one finds: *L'an mil sept cens feront grands emmenées*, 'The year seventeen hundred will see large migrations (or deportations)'. *Q71 (CVIII)* mentions *L'an mil six cens & sept par sacre glomes*, 'The year 1607 by sacred assemblies'. And *Q77 (CIII)* offers the predictive date: *Le tiers climat sous Aries comprins, l'an mil sept cens vingt & sept en Octobre*, 'The third climate included under Aries, the year one thousand, seven hundred and twenty-seven in October'.

Q71 (CVIII) is also worthy of note because of its reference to large numbers of astrologers who fall foul of the ecclesiastical establishment, a situation with which Nostradamus clearly felt at one, but the main concern must lie with the date:

Croistra le nombre si grande des astronomes
Chassez, bannis & liures censurez,
L'an mil six cens & sept par sacre glomes
Que nul aux sacres ne feront asseurez.

The number of astrologers will grow so great: hunted, banned and books censured by sacred assemblies in the year 1607, that none will be safe from the priests.

Do these various dates refer to the years 1607, 1700 and 1727, or to 2607, 2700 and 2727, or is there a degree of inconsistency? The outcome depends on whether Nostradamus adopted a style of dating whereby he discounted the period of Christianity prior to 1000 CE, or whether he was, indeed, concerned to achieve the closest to a decasyllabic scan, or whether he was merely inadvertently or deliberately untidy. These are questions to which we have no clear answers but it may be that several of the specific dates were inserted to provide no more than false trails.

Sometimes it would appear that commentators have detected a date to occur in a prediction when perhaps no such indication is present. An example is to be found in *Q51 (CII)* which has been seized on by several authors. If correct, their analysis would entirely throw the chronology argument. The putative date is delivered in the lines:

Le sang de juste à Londres de sera faulte
Brusles par fouldres de vingt trois les six:

The blood of just men will be demanded in London, six burnt by fires of twenty-three.

De vingt trois les six has been interpreted by several authors to refer to 666 or 1666 and therefore to provide a positive year date. This supposition, however, is extremely tenuous and the lines could offer an altogether different meaning, including any year date ending in 23 or no date at all.

If, however, we disregard the *Q51 (CII)* date as no more than a presumption by modern observers and take the *Q72 (CX)* date as being reliable, whilst also accepting that there is an onward chronological progression from the first to the last *quatrain*, a pattern emerges.

The *Q72 (CX)* date, along with those of *Q49 (CI)* and *Q54 (CVI)*, confirms that roughly three-quarters of each Century of 100 *quatrains* is concerned with the period from the date of composition, in about 1550, to the end of the twentieth century and that the balance of some 25–30 *quatrains* stretches out into the future, towards the ultimate end point predicted by Nostradamus to occur in the year 3797, taking into account the cumulative aberration brought by the reliance on the Julian calendar (see page 33). The failure of *Q77 (CIII)* to conform chronologically, irrespective of whether it refers to the year 1727 or 2727, may simply be an oversight or a false trail laid on the part of Nostradamus.

The 60 or so *quatrains* which apply to the second half of the twentieth century may now be searched in detail. Is it possible to set these against events taking place during this period? Playing devil's advocate, one prediction which stands as a potential obstacle to the systematic dating of the *quatrains* covering the second half of the twentieth century is that contained in **Q62 (CII)** because it describes the appearance of a comet when no actual astronomical record will ostensibly tally. The prophecy should, therefore, be examined carefully even though in terms of chronology it lies just outside the 50 year time-span of this chapter.

Mabus puis tost alors mourra viendra,
De gens & bestes une horrible defaite:
Puis tout à coup la vengeance on verra.
Cent, main, soif, faim, quand courra la comete.

Mabus (evil) will soon die and there will come a horrible destruction of humanity and beasts. Then a sudden retribution will come. Incoherent speeches, hands, thirst, hunger, when the comet will pass.

The *quatrain* provides great difficulty in translation because the word 'mabus' is incomprehensible unless a misprint for 'malus' meaning evil, and because of the vagueness of 'cent, main'. The Latin word 'cento' offers two distinct meanings. It implies both a numerical figure and incoherent speech or nonsense which, in itself, may provide a subtle clue to the overall meaning.

We should be looking for a predictive date of about 1940 but the chief difficulty lies in the absence of a major cometary appearance between November 1927 when 'Skjellerup-Maristany', a very bright body burning with an intense yellow light, became visible, and 1948 the year which marked the first sighting of the 'Eclipse Comet', recorded over east Africa.

The answer to this seeming aberration of chronology may lie in the portentous value of comets to herald future events. If we assume that the date of 1940 is fairly accurate then the prophecy clearly refers to Adolf Hitler, the evil man who brought such terrible destruction to Europe between 1939 and 1945 but who was destined soon to die by his own hand in the face of the rapid Allied advance and the taking of the German capital. One of Hitler's most notable attributes, from the outset of his rise to power, lay in his

EMACIATED SURVIVORS OF THE NAZI CONCENTRATION CAMP AT EVENSEE, VICTIMS OF THE EVIL IMPLIED IN *QUATRAIN* 62.

ability for powerful oratory, at times sufficiently rhetorical and impassioned that although the sentiment was extraordinarily vivid, the actual content verged on being nonsensical. Hitler was also fond of extravagant gestures of the hands whilst making his polemical speeches. His political and military adventures in Europe did indeed result in a period of great hunger and thirst as the holocaust took its toll and, subsequently, nations set about rebuilding their shattered infrastructure. Alternatively, 'a hundred (outstretched) hands' evokes powerful images of a starving populace and of the horrors of the concentration camps. But what of the significance of the comet?

This reference may be more pertinent than would appear at first glance when we investigate the historical significance of the year date. The year of the 'Skjellerup-Maristany' comet, 1927, marked the beginning of the economic crisis in Germany that provided the breeding ground in which Hitler's powers of persuasion and his Nazi propaganda machine were able to grow so successfully. The same year saw the disastrous withdrawal of the Allied Control Commission from Germany which allowed her to commence secret rearmament.

The crisis within German industry was to provide Hitler with the means to discredit political opposition. His National Socialist Party had already acquired a voice in government when, in the 1924 elections, it achieved its first gain of 33 parliamentary seats, and it was on the strength of Hitler's soaring popularity that the German president, Hindenburg, offered him the position of Reich Chancellor in 1933.

The inclusion of the comet in the prophecy is perhaps accurately retrospective, the *quatrain* thus encapsulating the beginning and end of Hitler's power in Europe.

Q63 (CIII) provides a fair reflection of the political situation in Italy around the time of the Second World War, reinforcing the claim that Nostradamus did not jumble his *quatrains* and that parallel *quatrain* 'series' from different Centuries draw us to the same time period.

Romain pouvoir sera du tout abas,
Son grand voisin initer les vestiges:
Occultes haines civiles & debats
Retarderont aux bouffons leurs folies.

The power of Rome will be brought down, in the footsteps of its great neighbour. Secret civil hatreds and disputes will delay the follies of the buffoons.

Before the Second World War Italy allied herself with the greater force of Germany as a key element of the Axis. Mussolini undoubtedly wished to tread in Hitler's footsteps and, in consequence, he was to bring Italy's power down. Both of the players, Hitler and Mussolini, developed and exhibited megalomania to a buffoonish degree and their conduct stirred up considerable hatred amongst their own compatriots.

Those selected *quatrains* serve as a useful prelude to the present era, suggesting that the hypothetical basis of dating which we have established is still working well. Moving forward to the 1950–1990 period itself, the first major conflict to take place was that of the Korean War which was waged from the summer of 1950 until the summer of 1953.

In **Q64 (CI)** Nostradamus introduces a vivid picture of aerial combat, a phenomenon wholly beyond his sixteenth-century experience, yet described even down to the small detail of pilots wearing snout-like oxygen masks:

De nuict soleil penseront avoir veu
Quand le pourceau demy homme on verra;
Bruict, chant, bataille, au ciel battre aperceu;
Et bestes brutes à parler lon orra.

At night they will imagine they have seen the sun, when the half pig-man is seen. Noise, cries, aerial battle. And dumb beasts will be heard to speak.

A sizeable part of the Korean war was fought in the skies with high-altitude jets. Much of modern warfare is also conducted at night and flares dropping out of the darkness do indeed make the sky appear lit up by the sun. The noise of aerial attack, coupled with the loudspeaker propaganda used by the North Koreans might well have been described as dumb beasts discovering the power of speech. Other *quatrains* seem to touch on details of the same conflict. **Q64 (CVI)** mentions a false peace and deceitfulness:

SABRE JETS OF THE US AIR FORCE'S 18TH FIGHTER-BOMBER WING WHICH WERE IN COMBAT WITH COMMUNIST MIG AIRCRAFT DURING THE KOREAN WAR.

On ne tiendra pache aucune arresté,
Tous recevans iront par tromperie:
De paix & tresue, terre & mer protesté
Par Barcelone classe prins d'industrie.

They will not maintain a peace agreed upon, and the
recipients will go to deceitful lengths. Of peace and truce,
land and sea have protested; the fleet is skilfully taken
by Barcelona.

During peace negotiations in the early part of 1953, the Chinese forces kept up their attacks and as late as two weeks before the July armistice was signed they launched a full divisional assault against the American forces holding the infamous Pork Chop Hill. Barcelona is perhaps no more than a generic term for a port since Nostradamus had little knowledge of the names of towns

and cities beyond Europe. In one of the greatest strategic master strokes of military history, the Americans had previously taken the port of Inchon which had enabled the recapture of Seoul and the severing of the supply route for the communist forces in the south.

Q61 (CII) describes the frustrated hopes of the peace-makers who comprised the Geneva Conference following the termination of hostilities in Korea under the armistice agreement of 1953. Discussion of the 1954 Geneva settlement plan was attended by representatives of the USA, the Soviet Union, France, the United Kingdom, the People's Republic of China and North and South Korea, but the conference ended without agreement.

After defeating the North Korean army, the commander of the UN forces, General Douglas MacArthur, had urged the use of the American naval force to attack mainland China but this was contrary to US

AMERICAN MARINES AWAIT ORDERS TO ADVANCE AFTER THEIR AMPHIBIOUS LANDING AT INCHON – A DECISIVE POINT
IN THE KOREAN WAR.

foreign policy and, in 1951, MacArthur was dismissed by the US President in office, Harry S. Truman.

Seicher de faim, de sois, gent Genevoise,
Espoir prochain viendra au defaillir,
Sur point tremblant fera loy Gebenoise.
Classe au grand port ne se peut acuillir.

Dried up by thirst and hunger, the next hopes of the people of Geneva will fail. The law of Gebenoise will be on the point of collapse. The fleet cannot be accepted at the great harbour.

Q65 (CVIII) seems to offer a remarkably accurate prediction of the internal Korean political scene at the time:

Le vieux frustré du principal espoir
Il parviendra au chef de son empire:
Vingt mois tiendra le regne à grand pouvoir,
Tiran, cruel en delaissant un pire.

The old man, frustrated in his main ambition, will become the leader of his empire. Twenty months will he rule with great force, a cruel tyrant who will give way to another, worse.

The President of South Korea from 1948 until 1960 was the much disliked and tyrannical Syngman Rhee. Born in 1875, he was an old man when fighting broke out in 1950 but, under the post-war US occupation, he claimed his government's right to rule over the whole of Korea. This ambition was thwarted some two years into his presidency when the communist-backed North Koreans invaded the South. North Korea was presided over by Kim Il Sung, who was arguably a far worse and a more despotic ruler than Rhee.

One of the other momentous events which preoccupied the world in the early 1950s was the Chinese overthrow of the remote mountain kingdom of Tibet and the exile of its spiritual leader, the Dalai Lama. **Q65 (CIV)** seems to predict the scenario well:

THE PRESIDENT OF SOUTH KOREA, SYNGMAN RHEE –ARGUABLY THE 'OLD MAN' OF Q65 (CVIII) – SEATED NEXT TO GENERAL MACARTHUR DURING THE CEREMONY PROCLAIMING KOREA A REPUBLIC IN 1948.

Au deserteur de la grand forteresse,

Apres qu'aura son lieu abandonné

Son adversaire fera si grand prouesse,

L'Empereur tost mort sera condamné.

To the deserter of the great fortress, when he will have abandoned his post, his adversary will show so great a prowess, the Emperor will be condemned to death.

The *quatrain* number, 65, indicates that we have reached the mid-1950s in the overall timescale. In 1949 the People's Republic of China encroached on Tibet's sovereignty and the Dalai Lama was forced to flee to India, abandoning his fortress-like Potala Palace high in the mountains at Lhasa. In 1954 Tibet was declared an autonomous region of China and by the end of that year the Chinese had consolidated their position in all except the Lhasa region. A further military incursion occurred in 1959 in response to a major Tibetan uprising. The Chinese usurped the old Tibetan culture, religion and ideology, and this period of turmoil was marked not only by considerable bloodshed but also by the forcible imposition of Marxist-Maoist philosophy which led to the destruction of nearly a thousand monasteries.

The Chinese authorities did not actually issue a death sentence *in absentia* against the Dalai Lama but they initiated a policy of downgrading his divinity and undermining his position as Tibet's spiritual leader, describing him as 'the head of a serpent which must be chopped off'.

Q66 (CII) appears also to describe the flight of the Dalai Lama and the miserable destiny of his monks left in Lhasa, with the royal palace surrounded on all sides by hostile Chinese forces.

Par grans dangiers le captif eschapé

Peu de temps grand à fortune changée

Dans le palais le peuple est attrapé

Par bon augure la cité assiegée.

In great dangers, the captive has escaped. In a little time, his fortune has changed greatly. In the palace the people are trapped, by good omen the city besieged.

THE DALAI LAMA IS GREETED BY OFFICIALS IN INDIA AFTER HIS ESCAPE, BY HORSE AND YAK-SKIN BARGE, FROM THE CHINESE INVASION OF TIBET.

The period spanned by *quatrain* 65 may, arguably, extend into the very early 1960s and if this range is accurate then **Q65 (CII)** displays considerable insight.

Le parc enclin grande calamité

Par l'Hesperie & Insubre fera

Le feu en nef peste & captivité

Mercure en l'arc Saturne fenera.

The half-hearted move towards great calamity, by the West and Lombardy. The fire in the ship, pestilence and captivity. Mercury in Sagittarius, Saturn threatening.

A notable assortment of translations has been rendered for the first line of this *quatrain* and, in fairness, it has to be treated to a degree of literary interpretation. Erika Cheetham offers: *In the feeble lists, great calamity.* Peter Lemesurier interprets the line as: *Thrift once abandoned, great calamity.* The word *parc* probably derives from the

Latin *parcus* meaning economical or frugal, although in modern French it sometimes means a fleet (of vehicles).

Let us disregard the astronomical conjunction which appears to be misleading, and also consider that the obscure reference to Lombardy may be no more than an allegory in that the Lombards once threatened the world order by marching on Rome. 1962 was the year of the Bay of Pigs fiasco when the United States attempted a 'calamitous' invasion of Cuba and many of the country's marines were captured. The action resulted in the Soviets sending a seaborne cargo of missiles to Cuba, the 'fire in the ship', which was intercepted by the American fleet and which brought the world to the brink of nuclear war.

At least one more revealing *quatrain* with the number 65 must be mentioned, **Q65 (CI)**:

> *Enfant sans mains jamais veu si grand foudre*
> *L'enfant royal au jeu d'oesteus blessé*
> *Au puy brises fulgures allant mouldre*
> *Trois souz les chaines par le milieu troussés.*

Child without hands, never witnessed so great a thunderbolt. The royal child injured in a game. At the well flashes of lightning strike, three with chains secured by the middle.

The final part of this *quatrain*, referring to three bound with chains, is difficult to decipher but, given the period of time and the references in the *quatrain* 66 series below, may conceivably allude to the three Kennedy brothers. The rest represents an astonishing piece of foresight on the part of a man who clearly had no medical knowledge of that dreadful affliction which was to come in his distant future.

In 1960 the pharmaceutical company William S. Merrell Co. of Cincinnati asked the American Food and Drug Administration to approve a product which had been developed under the trade name Kavadon. Already in use in Europe and Canada, in 1959 the drug, marketed as a safe sedative, had been launched in 48 countries. In the same year, however, 12 West German babies with

THE ENIGMATIC WORDS OF Q65 (CI) DESCRIBING 'THREE BOUND WITH CHAINS' COULD PLAUSIBLY ALLUDE TO THE KENNEDY BROTHERS, PHOTOGRAPHED HERE IN 1960.

truncated and malformed limbs were born to women who had used the drug during pregnancy. Its generic name was thalidomide and, by 1962 when it was taken off the market, between 10,000 and 12,000 babies had been born with limbs missing or severely deformed. About half the number had died in infancy.

To a person living in the religious climate of the sixteenth century, even one versed in the medicine of his day, this kind of affliction would have been seen as a thunderbolt from heaven, a lightning strike of divine wrath. It must be probable that at least one infant of a royal household, whose fate was not reported, was born afflicted with thalidomide impairment during the brief period of the drug's marketing. (Thalidomide is now, incidentally, making a medical comeback in the treatment of HIV, certain types of ulcer and some brain cancers.)

A remarkably accurate prophecy concerning a different issue occurs in **Q66** (**CX**):

Le chef de Londres par regne l'Americh,
L'isle d'Escosse tempiera par gellée
Roy Reb auront un si faux antechrist
Que les mettra trestous dans la meslée.

The London premier by American power, will impose on the island of Scotland a cold thing. Reb, the king, will have an antichrist so dreadful that it will bring difficulties to them all.

The period of *quatrain* 66 is the early 1960s. The British premier at that time was Harold Macmillan and it was his responsibility to invite the American Polaris submarine fleet, the 'cold [war] thing' as Nostradamus describes it, to Faslane on the river Clyde.

There exists an entertaining possibility concerning the third line of the prediction. In the United States the early 1960s marked the rise to unprecedented fame of a child of the deep 'rebel' south. Elvis Aaron Presley became known to his adoring followers as 'the king' and, to many, he was probably the epitome of the antichrist! There is, however, a more sober alternative explanation for the reference to the king and the antichrist. One is, inevitably, drawn to search Nostradamus' prophecies for

the untimely death of one of the most notable and charismatic statesmen of the era, John Fitzgerald Kennedy, assassinated by Lee Harvey Oswald, in Dallas, Texas, on 22 November 1963. To many of Kennedy's followers he was revered as a king and Oswald must also have seemed to be the antichrist incarnate.

There is a further allusion to the Kennedy assassination, though with some confusing aspects, contained in **Q66** (**CIII**):

Le grand Baillif d'Orléans mis à mort,
Sera par un de sang vindicatif.
De mort merite ne mourra, ne par sort,
Des pieds & mains malle faisoit captif.

The great bailiff of Orléans put to death. It will be by one who is vindictive for his blood. He will not die a deserved death, nor one by his jurors. Hands and feet will be poorly tied.

Nostradamus would not have been acquainted with the name Dallas but perhaps he has offered us an American city of the southern states whose title, New Orleans, was copied from one with which he was certainly familiar. Once more, in apparent echoes of **Q65** (**CI**), there emerges, in this *quatrain*, a reference to tying or binding with chains. It is a fair observation, in this respect, that some of Kennedy's policies, both domestic and foreign, were restricted, his 'hands and feet tied' by conservative elements within the United States. His critics saw moves towards racial integration at home, and the easing of east-west tensions abroad, as liberalization gone too far. Speculation has been rife in the years since Kennedy's death that it was his liberal stance which led to his death and, later, to the assassination of his brother Robert.

Moving forward in time, the Six Day Arab-Israeli War of 1967 appears to be the subject of **Q67** (**CII**):

Le blonde au nez forche viendra commettre
Par le duelle chassera dehors;
Les exilés dedans sera remettre
Aux lieux marins commettant les plus fors.

78

PRESIDENT JOHN F. KENNEDY'S LAST MOMENTS AS HE RIDES THROUGH DALLAS, TEXAS: HIS ASSASSINATION SHOOK THE WORLD AND APPEARS TO HAVE BEEN FORESEEN BY NOSTRADAMUS.

The fair-skinned man will engage the hook-nosed one in

combat and will drive him out. He will restore the exiles,

placing the strongest close to the sea.

The Israeli commander, Major-General Yeshayahu Gavish, the fair-skinned man, drove out the hook-nosed Egyptian General Abd el Mohsen Mortagy and destroyed his army, establishing a strong defence line along the sea channel of the Suez Canal and restoring the security of the 'exiles', a time-honoured title for the people of Israel, derived from the biblical account of the Exodus.

Q67 (CIV) describes the appearance of a comet with its predictive dating more or less exact, given that the *quatrain* number takes the period to the late 1960s:

L'an que Saturne & Mars esgaux combust,

L'air fort seiché longue traiection

Par feux secrets, d'ardeur grand lieu adust

Peu pluye, vent chault, guerres, incursions.

The year that Saturn and Mars are equally fiery, the

air is very dry; a long trajectory {comet}. By the hidden

fires, a great place burns fiercely. Scant rain, hot wind,

wars, incursions.

Comet Bennett was discovered in December 1969 and could be seen with the naked eye in the southern hemisphere in February 1970, becoming visible in northern latitudes by the middle of March. The

observation of dry air, hot wind, wars and incursions may well also refer to the Six Day War.

It is fascinating to discover a detailed reference to famine within this particular period. *Q67 (CI)* indicates that starvation is approaching on a global scale:

La grande famine que je sens approcher
Souvent tourner, puis estre universelle:
Si grande & longue qu'on viendra arracher
Du bois racine, & l'enfant de mammelle.

The great famine that I feel approaches will often appear
virtually global. So great will it be over such a long time
that people will forage roots from trees and take children
from the breast.

Israeli troops, occupying Bethlehem during the Six Day War of 1967, pause in the square beside the Church of the Nativity, built over the traditional birthplace of Jesus.

This is a dire predictive warning of the growing reality of famine on a global scale, a prospect which was heeded, significantly, in the early 1960s when the British-based Oxford Committee for Famine Relief expanded to become a major international non-governmental aid organization. Its founders had recognized the urgent need to address the fundamental causes of poverty and to tackle the growing incidence of malnourishment or starvation, particularly in sub-Saharan Africa where the environmental situation was beginning to reveal the signs of impending catastrophe.

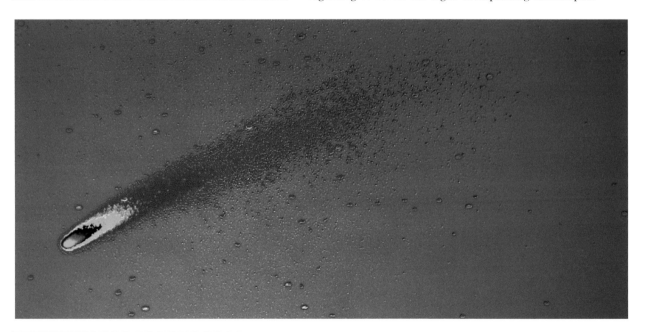

Comet Bennett became visible in 1970. Its dramatic appearance is here enhanced by isophote mapping, which translates shades of grey into selected colours.

Subsequent chronic famines in Ethiopia, Sudan and other neighbouring regions suggests that the alarm was justified and the response well-timed.

Another *quatrain* in the '67 series' predicting events in and around the close of the 1960s is **Q67** (***CIII***) and, once again, Nostradamus renders a prophecy of sobering astuteness.

> *Une nouvelle secte de Philosophes,*
> *Mesprisant mort, or, honneurs & richesses:*
> *Des monts Germains ne seront limitrophes,*
> *A les ensuyure auront appuy & presses.*

> *A new sect of philosophers, despising death, gold, honours*
> *and riches, will not be limited to the German mountains.*
> *Amongst their following there will be support and crowds.*

The year of 1968 brought a new and terrifying phenomenon to the Federal Republic of Germany in the shape of three extreme left-wing socialist revolutionaries who believed that post-war Germany had become a capitalism-orientated fascist state. The trio included Andreas Baader, Ulrike Meinhof and Gudrun Ensslin who, together, became the founder-members of the Baader-Meinhof gang, more formally titled the Red Army Faction. Sister terrorist groups included West Berlin Tupamaros, the Socialist Patients Collective, Movement 2 June and Revolutionary Cells. The groups, committed to the violent overthrow of capitalist society, expanded until about 1977 and then declined in activity. Baader and Meinhof both died in prison but during the period between 1968 and 1977 they executed numerous acts of terrorism both in and beyond the frontiers of Germany.

From time to time it may appear that Nostradamus has predicted actual events with great foresight but has erred slightly in his chronology. It is, however, all too easy to make hasty criticism of his prophecies for being sited early or late, when closer inspection reveals that it

MASKED SYMPATHIZERS DISPLAY A BANNER IN STUTTGART'S DARNHALDEN CEMETERY AFTER THE SUICIDE AND BURIAL OF THREE OF
THE LEADERS OF THE BAADER-MEINHOF GANG.

is *we* who are guilty of misinterpretation. Even when Nostradamus seems fairly to have been a decade or so adrift in his prognostication one should consider what an astonishing achievement that level of accuracy sometimes presents.

Q65 (**CIX**) offers a good illustration of the pitfalls awaiting us. The *quatrain* should, according to the timescale, be predicting events in the latter part of the 1950s or early 60s yet it includes, succinctly, an event of the most momentous importance for mankind which took place a decade later. When properly considered, however, the *quatrain* actually provides an extraordinarily accurate overview of the American space programme which began in 1961 and reached its first climax in 1969.

Dans le coing de luna viendra rendre,
Ou sera prins & mys en terre estrange
Les fruitz immeurs seront à grand esclandre
Grand vitupere à l'un grande louange.

One will be placed in the corner of the moon where he will be in a strange land. The immature fruit will be a great scandal. Great blame to the one, great praise {to the other}.

Nostradamus anticipated the breath-catching moment in July 1969 when Neil Armstrong became the first human being to set foot, stepping down from the landing craft of *Apollo 11*, on to the extraterrestrial lunar landscape. The chronology of his prediction is much more accurate than it seems on first inspection because it was a decade earlier, in 1961, that John F. Kennedy announced the plan to put Americans on the moon before 1970. The preliminary manned Mercury and Gemini flights took place between 1961 and 1966.

It seems clear that, when he referred to the 'immature fruit' which generated great scandal, Nostradamus was anticipating the near-catastrophe which was to follow with the systems failure of *Apollo 13* in April 1970, and the tragedy of 1986 when the space shuttle *Challenger* blew up during its ascent from Cape Canaveral, killing its entire crew and putting the American space effort on hold. Those incidents caused

NOSTRADAMUS CLEARLY FORESAW, OVER 400 YEARS INTO THE FUTURE, THE FIRST LANDING ON THE MOON, FOLLOWED BY THE NEAR-DISASTER OF APOLLO 13, SEEN HERE BLASTING OFF FROM CAPE KENNEDY.

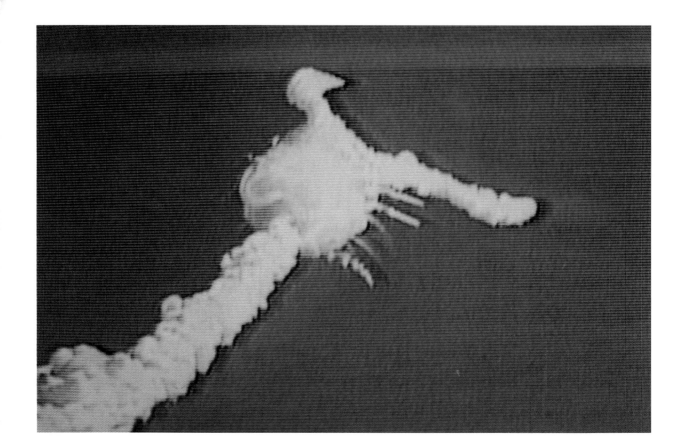

THE SPACE SHUTTLE CHALLENGER EXPLODES 72 SECONDS AFTER LIFT-OFF, KILLING ALL SEVEN ASTRONAUTS ON BOARD.

great blame to be attached to some and an equal measure of praise to be levelled elsewhere.

It is difficult to avoid the conclusion that the Falklands War of 1982 between Britain and Argentina is predicted in at least two of the *quatrain 68* series although, according to the timescale, one would have hoped to find the Falklands conflict referred to amongst the *quatrains* numbered 69. **Q68 (CX)** predicts:

L'armee de mer devant cité tiendra
Puis partira sans faire longue alée,
Citoyens grande proye en terre prendra
Retourner classe reprendre grand emblée.

The army of the sea will stand before the city, then depart without making a long passage. A great prey of citizens will be taken on land. The fleet returns to take back a great theft.

The Argentine navy brought a force of troops to occupy Port Stanley, capital of the Falkland Islands, without the necessity to embark on a long sea voyage. The British citizens of the islands were effectively made captives until the British fleet returned to the south Atlantic and recovered the 'great theft' of British sovereignty.

Another *quatrain* of the same series which seems to corroborate and follow on from the above is that of **Q68 (CII)**:

De l'aquilon les effors seront grands.
Sus l'ocean sera la porte ouverte
Le regne en l'isle sera reintegrand,
Tremblera Londres par voille descouverte.

In the north, the effort will be great. Over the ocean the port will be opened. Rule in the island will be re-established. London will fear the fleet when it is discovered.

The strenuous military preparations in Britain resulted in the liberation of Port Stanley and the restoration of British colonial rule in the Falklands. It is also an accurate forecast that one of the concerns of the London war office was the strength of the Argentine navy and the need to 'draw its teeth'.

It is intriguing to note the subsequent *quatrain*, *Q69* (*CX*), because it refers to a shining hero, exalted in the north and the south, who is slain. Lieutenant Colonel H. Jones, the commanding officer of the British land forces, having made the 'great journey', was killed at Goose Green in May 1982, whilst mounting an assault on an enemy position.

Le fait luysant de neuf vieux esleue
Seront si grand par midi aquilon,
De sa seur propre grande alles leue
Fuyant murdry au buysson d'ambellon.

The shining example of the new old exalted will be so great in south and north. Raised by his own sister, a great journey arises. Those fleeing commit murder in the bushes at ambellon.

The final line of the prophecy is hard to decipher since the word 'ambellon' has no immediate significance, though it may be derived in some way from 'bellos' reflecting war.

Nostradamus may be observing tersely that the killers of Lieutenant Colonel Jones were in retreat through the stunted scrub growth of the island.

Nostradamus also has shrewdly pertinent observations to make, in the *quatrain* 69 series, on aggressive happenings elsewhere in the world. *Q69* (*CV*) relates specifically to events taking place in Africa:

Plus ne sera le grand en faux sommeil
L'inquietude viendra prendre repoz:
Dresser phalange d'or, azur & vermeil,
Subjuger Affrique la ronger jusques oz.

No more will the great one remain asleep. Anxiety will take over from complacency: a phalanx of gold, blue and vermilion will be drawn up to subdue Africa and gnaw at its bones.

The only national colours flying in Africa and corresponding to 'gold, blue and vermilion' are those of the vast, land-locked Republic of Chad in the north and centre of the continent. The period of the *quatrain* is that taken up by the early 1980s and this also marked serious

A SOMBRE IMAGE OF WAR: THE HELMETS OF ARGENTINE TROOPS LIE SCATTERED AFTER THE BATTLE OF GOOSE GREEN IN THE FALKLAND ISLANDS.

military disturbance in Chad. Originally part of colonial French Equatorial Africa, the country achieved independence in 1960, but in 1982 a transitional government led by President Goukouni Oueddei was ousted by rebel forces under Hissene Habré. The capital, N'djamena, was overrun and Habré assumed the presidency. Fighting then broke out again in 1983 between the opposing forces of Oueddei and Habré. By this juncture Oueddei was backed by Libyan arms and money, whilst the Chad government forces, under Habré, were being actively supported by France. Arguably, in terms of Nostradamus' prophecy, France was 'the great one' no longer prepared to sleep complacently whilst her ex-colony descended into anarchy and civil war. Political instability had also plagued Chad throughout much of the 1960s and 70s and, in consequence, her economy had suffered major depletion. Nostradamus describes the situation poetically as 'gnawing at Africa's bones'.

A no less revealing insight into Nostradamus' astute perception is contained in *Q70 (CVIII)*:

Il entera vilain, meschant, infame
Tyrannisant la Mesopotamie,
Tous amys fait d'adulterine d'ame.
Tertre horrible noir de phisonomie.

He will enter, villainous, wicked, infamous, tyrannising Mesopotamia. All friends made of the adulterous woman. Land horrible and blackened of aspect.

The approximate dating which must be attributed to the *quatrain* 70 series is the late 1980s. In 1980 the newly elected President of Iraq, Saddam Hussein, declared war against his neighbour in Mesopotamia, Iran. The ensuing conflict was bloody in the extreme and persisted for eight years until an uneasy truce was obtained in 1988. It is, however, the last line of the *quatrain* which offers the most fascinating reading. In 1990 Saddam Hussein, still keen for military conquest, followed up his war with Iran by invading the small neighbouring country of Kuwait. By deliberately setting fire to the

THE BODIES OF SOLDIERS LIE WHERE THEY FELL – VICTIMS OF CONFLICT IN THE CENTRAL AFRICAN REPUBLIC OF CHAD IN THE EARLY 1980S.

AMERICAN MARINES SILHOUETTED AGAINST THE BILLOWING SMOKE OF KUWAIT'S BURNING OIL WELLS — A 'HORRIBLE, BLACKENED' LAND.
INSET: SADDAM HUSSEIN AT AN EMERGENCY ARAB SUMMIT IN BAGHDAD. IS HE THE TYRANT REFERRED TO IN *QUATRAIN* 70?

nation's oil wells, he made the land truly 'horrible and blackened of aspect'. As far as the reference to adultery goes, it was rumoured that Saddam enjoyed the favours of a long-term mistress in addition to his legal wife, formerly one Miss Tofy.

This prediction tallies extraordinarily well with that of *Q70 (CI)* which seems to describe the situation in neighbouring Iran:

> *Pluie, faim, guerre en Perse non cessée,*
> *La foy trop grand trahira le monarque:*
> *Par la finie en Gaule commencée,*
> *Secret augure pour à un estre parque.*

> *Rain, famine, war without ceasing in Persia. The trust too great will betray the king. By the end, that commenced in France will result in a secret treaty for one person to be moderate.*

The Ayatollah Khomeini was the other major protagonist in the eight-year war between Iraq and Iran which, through most of its course, was largely stalemated and must have seemed never-ending in the eyes of the combatants. As leader of Iran's revolution, Khomeini had taken over the country in 1979 and his extremist policies had, for some time, thrown the country's economy into turmoil, resulting in considerable hardship for the mass of the population. Prior to his return from years of exile in France, Khomeini had plotted his revenge against the Persian monarchy from Paris, hence the French connection mentioned in the *quatrain*. In Paris, Khomeini had promulgated his vision of Iran as an 'Islamic Republic'. The 'trust too great' was undoubtedly that which the Shah placed in his American backers who regarded him as a staunch anti-communist ally and a valuable stabilizing influence in the Middle East. What had been catastrophically underestimated by the Americans was the depth of antagonism to the Shah's autocratic and corrupt regime within almost every strand of Persian society.

The conclusion of the Iran-Iraq War took the form of an uneasy truce and although Iran maintained a level of peaceful moderation, Iraq was then to turn its aggressive interests in the direction of its smaller and infinitely more vulnerable neighbour.

Elsewhere in the world Nostradamus seems to have

had his finger on the pulse of momentous events taking place in the late 1980s with no less accuracy. The years 1989 and 1990 witnessed a number of communist regimes in eastern Europe giving way to more democratic governments. Most of these power shifts took place amidst comparative calm, though peaceful transition was not the case in Romania. The regime of her dictator, Nicolae Ceausescu, was terminated in December 1989 but only after a particularly bloody two-week civil war which claimed many thousands of lives including those of Ceausescu and his wife Elena. Many people, in a country where religion had been cruelly suppressed, saw the execution of the Ceausescus as a divine retribution and *Q70 (CII)* articulates this punishment as 'an arrow from heaven':

> Le dard du ciel fera son estendue
> Mors en parlant: grand execution:
> Le pierre en l'arbre la fière gent rendue
> Bruit humain monstre purge expiation.

> The celestial arrow will travel his path. Death while speaking, a great execution. The stone in the tree, the proud nation brought down. The rumour of a human monster, purge, expiation.

Ceausescu was, figuratively, the cancer or 'stone' in the body politic of Romania who had brought a proud nation low. Having taken power in 1968, he held office for longer than any other communist leader in eastern Europe and, during his time, he ruthlessly suppressed opposition whilst indulging himself and his family in an opulent lifestyle. To the very end he had browbeaten and cajoled the Romanian people to remain loyal to his autocratic regime but, after the December riots which resulted in the death of many unarmed civilians, he and his wife were captured whilst trying to flee the country. The couple were executed by firing squad on Christmas Day 1989 and eventually the country was purged of its old Ceausescu supporters, including the so-called National Salvation Front, though this did not happen until the elections of 1996 took place.

Q70 (CVI) appears to predict a dominant and charismatic personality who was to reach the world stage during the 1980s. In 1981 Ronald Reagan assumed the Republican presidency of the United States, having served as Governor of California. This remarkable man had risen from the ranks of unmemorable film actor to the highest office of government and such was his success on the world stage that there are now serious moves afoot to have

THE ROMANIAN PRESIDENT, NICOLAE CEAUSESCU, WAS EXECUTED BY FIRING SQUAD AFTER THE COLLAPSE OF HIS DICTATORSHIP.

PRESIDENT OF THE UNITED STATES DURING THE 1980S, RONALD REAGAN BECAME A SIGNIFICANT FIGURE IN THE MOVES TO END THE COLD WAR, THOUGH 'INITIALLY DISREGARDED' AS THE PROPHECY SAYS.

his profile carved into the heights of Mount Rushmore National Memorial in South Dakota to accompany those of Washington, Jefferson, Lincoln and Theodore Roosevelt. It was Reagan's characteristic mix of charm, ease of communication, toughness and passionate belief in the superiority of capitalism and democracy, the 'American way', over that of communism which led him to be, as the *quatrain* indicates, 'more loved and feared'. It provided for his rapport with Soviet leaders, which paved the way for the ending of the cold war and the ultimate

collapse of the communist dream, leaving America to rule the world stage.

> *Au chef du monde le grand Chyren sera*
> *Plus oultre apres aymé, craint, redoubté:*
> *Son bruit & loz les cieux surpassera,*
> *Et du seul victeur fort contenté.*

> *The great 'Chyren' will lead the world, after initial*
> *disregard {he will be} more loved, feared, dreaded: his*
> *sound and fame will surpass the heavens and he will*
> *content himself with the title of supremo.*

Several authors have puzzled over the word 'Chyren' but it is perhaps no more obscure than an awkward spelling of

CHILDREN HOLD THEIR NOSES AS THEY PASS DEAD BODIES NEAR A REFUGEE CAMP IN ZAIRE, WHERE THEY HAVE FLED
FROM THE GENOCIDE IN RWANDA.

Chiron, the fabulous *centaur* of Greek legend who was not only renowned for his wisdom but was also well disposed towards humankind.

The next *quatrain* to be examined takes us into the first half-decade of the 1990s. *Q71 (CIV)* is perhaps not correct in all its details but its prophetic accuracy is chilling:

> *En lieu d'espouse les filles trucidées,*
> *Meurte à grande faulte ne sera superstile*
> *Dedans le puys vestules inondées,*
> *L'espouse estaincte par hauste d'Aconite.*

> *Instead of the wife the girls are slaughtered, murder so evil, it will not be surpassed. Vestals are drowned in wells, the wife slain by Aconite poison.*

In April and May of 1994 one of the most horrendous incidents of genocide, unsurpassed in modern times, took place in Rwanda when over half a million Tutsi and moderate Hutus were killed. It has been noted by UN special investigator reports that women, especially, were the targets of torture and massacre. According to subsequent calculations between a quarter and half a million rapes took place during the period of genocide, many involving young girls. According to Amnesty International, Catholic nuns or 'vestals' were also particularly singled out for killing. The references to drowning and poisoning cannot be verified since most of the attacks were carried out with rifles or machetes but clearly those favoured for abuse would have been younger women and girls rather than matrona.

It is also perhaps worth pointing out, within the European context, that in July of 1995 the Bosnian Serb capture of Srebrenica resulted in the flight of some 12,000 Muslims to Tuzla, of whom less than half are believed to have reached safety. The remainder were victims of the worst genocide atrocities committed in Europe since the Second World War, according to UNHCR. It has to be said, however, that the victims of this massacre comprised almost exclusively male refugees.

Another *quatrain* from the 71 series imparts a prognostication on a separate aspect of the war in the

Balkans. *Q71 (CI)* describes an attack on a coastal citadel:

La tour marine trois fois prise & reprise,
Par Hespagnols, Barbares, Ligurins:
Marseilles & Aix, Arles par ceux de Pise,
Vast, feu, fer, pillé Avignon des Thurins.

The marine fortification, three times captured and recaptured, by Spanish, Barbarians and Ligurians. Marseilles, Aix and Arles by those of Pisa. Laying waste by fire, sword and pillage Avignon by the forces of Turin.

One may perhaps dispense here with all the specific details of towns and countries since those listed must be regarded as a reflection on the limitations of Nostradamus' dictionary. Suffice to observe that there are many nationalities involved in the conflict described; in other words, a multinational force is taking part in the action.

In 1992 the ancient fortified coastal city of Dubrovnik was attacked for at least the third time since the mid-sixteenth century. The most recent incursion hitherto had been conducted in 1807 when a joint Montenegran-Russian force failed to oust a French colonial occupation under Napoleon. Early in 1992 the Yugoslav People's Army started shelling Dubrovnik from inland. The siege lasted for six months until the attackers were obliged to call off their action under the threat of a UN intervention and whilst the eyes of the world rested on the plight of the city.

The 72 series of *quatrains* brings us to the second half of the 1990s and to the present day. Most of these prophecies appear, on first impression, to be couched in fairly obtuse terms and therefore they demand a more thorough degree of research.

Nostradamus interpreters have described *Q72 (CIII)* as being obscure and some have even dispensed with it as a 'failed *quatrain*', yet when placed in the time period it becomes decipherable.

Le bon veillart tout vif enseuely,
Près du grand fleuve par fausse souspeçon
Le nouveau vieux de richesse ennobly,
Prins à chemin tout l'or de la rançon.

THOUSANDS MARCH THROUGH TUZLA TO DEMAND THAT A SEARCH BE MADE TO FIND 7000 MEN MISSING FROM SREBRENICA, ONE OF THE WORST-HIT AREAS IN THE WAR IN FORMER YUGOSLAVIA.

The good old man, all alive by false superstition, is buried near the great river. The new old man, ennobled by riches, has taken the ransom money on the way.

On 19th February 1997 the Chinese communist party leader Deng Xiao Ping died at the age of 92 after a slow terminal decline in his health. In his final years, in order to maintain political stability in China, based on the superstitious belief of the populace in Deng's inviolability, he was virtually kept alive on a day-to-day basis by his team of physicians and he was, to all intent and purpose, an illustration of the 'living dead'. His funeral took place in Beijing and his ashes were scattered, not in China's great Yellow River, the Huang He, but, in accordance with his family's wishes, at sea.

DENG XIAO PING, LEADER OF THE CHINESE COMMUNIST PARTY, IN THE FOREGROUND OF A GROUP OF SWIMMERS. IT IS NOT IMPROBABLE THAT HE WAS 'THE GOOD OLD MAN' KEPT 'ALIVE BY FALSE SUPERSTITION'.

Deng was a reformer and a modernizer who was faced with making political and practical reparations in the aftermath of the chaos brought by Mao Tse Tung's more extreme ideologies. Notwithstanding his involvement in authorizing the Tiananmen Square massacre, he was generally looked upon, both at home and abroad, as a good man.

In his wake the aged president, Jiang Zemin, is now believed to favour the amendment of the Chinese communist party constitution to reinstate the position of party chairman since Jiang wishes to be appointed to this office. In a power move which will greatly enhance his stature, the party general secretary will then become his subordinate. As to riches and ransom money taken along the way, the great prize handed to China in 1997 has been that of the capitalist jewel of affluence, Hong Kong.

Q72 (CV) also seems to reflect the life and love of a personality whose loss was felt worldwide in 1997.

> Pour le plaisir d'edict voluptueux,
> On meslera la poyson dans l'aloy:
> Venus sera en cours si virtueux,
> Qu'obfusquera du soleil tout a loy.

For the pleasures of sensual nature, poison and fidelity are mixed. At court, Venus will be so pure, that all the glory of the sun will be obscured by her.

Diana, Princess of Wales, possessed the beauty of a Venus, eclipsing all around her and she was the darling of the world's press. Whilst in the eyes of the public she was virtuous and could do little wrong, in Dodi Fayed she sought more hedonistic pleasures away from the glare of the media and in escape from the ongoing misery of her recent divorce from Prince Charles. In the closing of her brief moments of fidelity to a man she had known for only a few weeks, a hotel chauffeur, fuelled on the 'poison' of alcohol, was to steer her car, fatally and at high speed, into a concrete pillar in a Paris underpass beside the Seine.

The circumstance, and an alleged cause of Charles and Diana's marital breakdown is perhaps also alluded to in **Q72 (CVI)**:

> Par fureur faincte d'esmotion divine,
> Sera la femme du grand fort violée:
> Juges voulans damner telle doctrine
> Victime au peuple ignorant imolée.

DIANA, PRINCESS OF WALES, ARRIVING AT THE SERPENTINE GALLERY IN LONDON FOR A GALA DINNER IN 1994: THE 'VENUS AT COURT' OF QUATRAIN 72 (CV)?

Through the feigned passion of divine emotion the wife of the great one will be strongly violated. Judges wishing to condemn such doctrine, the victim is sacrificed {immolated} to ignorant people.

The close friend of Prince Charles, Camilla Parker-Bowles, a wife in all but name who now reigns as mistress in his country home of Highgrove, has aroused strong adverse passions and she has been perceived, amongst the British public, to have violated the matrimonial position of Diana. She has been castigated in a manner that few other women in the public eye have experienced in recent times. Her possible future role as wife of Charles has been thwarted, or sacrificed, to the opinions of those whom the heir to the throne would probably regard as ignorant people.

One of the most intriguing amongst the 72 series of predictions is the prophecy contained in **Q72 (CIX)**. It is a *quatrain* which one must read, before any sense can be made of its veiled message, with a renewed awareness of the limited dictionary that Nostradamus had at his disposal in the mid-sixteenth century, and in sympathy with his comparatively limited experiences of the wider world.

Encor seront les saincts temples pollus,
Et expillez par Senat Tholossain,
Saturne deux trois cicles revollus,
Dans Avril, May, gens de nouveau levain.

Again the holy places will be desecrated and plundered by the Senate of Toulouse. Saturn having completed two or three cycles, in April and May people of a new leaven.

Putting aside the reference to the cycles of Saturn, which is fairly non-specific and therefore probably misleading, the remainder of the *quatrain* presents a fairly authentic picture of a sequence of bloody events which took place in the Arab world in 1997. At least three notable atrocities occurred, all accompanied by considerable loss of life and all carried out against the established order by religious fanatics, the new creed or 'leaven' of Islamic fundamentalists.

The first incident took place in Upper Egypt in the city of Abo-Korkas where, on 12th February, an Islamic group entered the Coptic Christian church and murdered 15 youths. It has been said that the Egyptian authorities did little to seek out and arrest the perpetrators.

The next incident, of greater severity, occurred in Algeria early in the morning of 29th August when Islamic fundamentalists butchered at least 300 people to death. This followed an atrocity earlier in the same week when some 200 unarmed civilians were slain. The attacks were symptomatic of a chronic ongoing unrest in the aftermath of refusal by the army-backed government of Algeria to impose the general election of 1992 in which the radical Islamic party were clear front-runners. The violence had accelerated since June of 1997 when a newly elected

SURVIVORS HELP TO IDENTIFY BODIES AFTER THE MASSACRE OF 300 VILLAGERS IN ALGERIA IN 1997.

government came to office with the promise to put an end to the terrorist attacks. During the assault on three hamlets south of Algiers, churches were ransacked and victims were decapitated or had their throats slit.

The third notable massacre which, like that in Abo-Korkas, involved a temple, though one of very different age and creed, took place near Luxor in Egypt on 19th November when 58 holidaymakers were murdered by Islamic fanatics. The tourists were visiting the ruins of the ancient Temple of Queen Hatshepsut when about ten gunmen approached the site and opened fire without warning. Having killed two security guards they approached the temple steps, crowded with sightseers, and opened fire at random. Many of the victims first fled into the temple complex where they became trapped and were mown down by machine-gun bullets. In the battle which ensued between the terrorists and police, six gunmen were killed.

We are left, in this *quatrain*, with the puzzling reference to plunder by the 'Senate of Toulouse' and it is here that we need to understand the way in which, at times, Nostradamus resorted to allegory when he did not have the words at his disposal to describe accurately events destined to take place far beyond his own time. In this particular instance he had no ready means of

articulating the spectre of Islamic militant terrorist groups engaging in acts of violence against the established order.

In order to decipher the meaning of the Senate of Toulouse we must reach back deeply into history. At the onset of the fifth century CE the world order was effectively that of Rome. The empire was eroding but Rome was still the *force majeure* in Europe and Rome represented the establishment. In 410 CE, however, Rome fell, with great bloodshed, to the Visigoth army of Alaric. The Visigoths were a branch of the Germanic tribes which had originated in Scandinavia and whose short-lived empire was destroyed by the Huns and Franks. The sack of Rome by Alaric was viewed by her citizens as the rape of civilization by a barbarian horde bringing with them alien culture and foreign gods. The connection between Toulouse and barbarians assaulting the established order only becomes apparent when one learns that, after the sack of Rome, the Visigoths invaded Gaul, setting up their capital and seat of government in the city of Toulouse. Nostradamus was familiar with the history of the Visigoths and of Toulouse, which was once also the capital of Aquitaine, since he refers to the subject in several other *quatrains*.

We need to appreciate that, having reached the time period represented by the 72 series of *quatrains*, we have entered not only the immediate past and present, but also the immediate future. It may be expected, therefore, that **Q72 (CIX)** may also deliver a projection of similar events to take place in the next two or three years.

Of all the *quatrains* in the 72 series it is, however, the celebrated prophecy of Century X which has received the most attention. Its prediction has provided abundant pen-fodder for interpreters of Nostradamus, not least amongst them the doomsday lobby, and it has prompted a convenient link to be contrived between this *quatrain* and a key observation in the letter to Nostradamus' son and heir, César.

Q72 (CX) runs as follows:

> *L'an mil neuf cent nonante neuf sept mois,*
> *Du ciel viendra un grand Roy d'effrayeur*
> *Ressusciter le grand Roy d'Angoulmois,*
> *Avant après Mars regner par bonheur.*

> *In July 1999, a great and terrifying ruler will come from the skies and revive the great king of the Angoulmois before and after which Mars will rule with fortune.*

It has been fashionable to treat the *quatrain* as an emphatic prophecy of the 'beginning of the end', the apocalyptic close of the millennium and the conclusion of the Piscean Age. Apart from the clear dating, the key elements include the mention of the king of the Angoulmois, the reference to his arrival from the skies, and the allusion to the warlike character of Mars.

As we saw in Chapter 1, this *quatrain* offers one of the best illustrations of how writers on Nostradamus are tempted to interpret his words according to the theory they have in mind. We should look at the popular interpretation again before going on to consider other possibilities.

Angoulmois is generally considered to refer to a clan based around the locality of Angoulême, a town in south-west France, and in fact Nostradamus refers to Angoulême in several other prophecies. The Angoulmois, it is argued popularly, were once conquered by the Visigoths described above and their land was subsequently invaded by the Mongol-derived Huns under the command of Attila. The 'coming from the skies', coupled with the reference to Mars, has therefore been interpreted to

define an airborne invasion of France from the east in July 1999. One variation on the argument, already mentioned, which asserts that Angoulmois also provides an anagram of Mongolois, seems particularly tenuous.

In historical reality the Visigoths were forced across the Danube by the Huns in 376 CE, first establishing themselves in the Balkans, then taking Rome, before moving into France and Spain. The Visigoths ruled initially as Roman subjects and then independently, but their rule in south-west France was destroyed, not by the Huns who had indeed occupied other parts of Gaul in the late fourth and fifth centuries, but by the Franks in 507 CE.

It is important never to lose sight of the fact that Nostradamus was a seer whose experience was limited to sixteenth-century France and whose prophecies were also destined to be used as a political football. The interesting mention of the 'grand Roy d'Angoulmois' may in truth be a reference not to an earlier ruler but to an illegitimate son of Charles IX. Born in 1573, seven years after the death of Nostradamus, he was afforded the title of Charles de

ATTILA, LEADER OF THE HUNS, IS HAILED BY HIS PEOPLE AFTER THEIR CONQUEST OF HUNGARY. SOME WRITERS HAVE INTERPRETED 'ANGOULMOIS' IN Q72 (CX) AS AN ANAGRAM OF MONGOLOIS AND THUS MADE A CONNECTION WITH THE MONGOL ORIGINS OF THE HUNS.

THE WELL-KNOWN *QUATRAIN* 72 MIGHT MORE PLAUSIBLY REFER TO CHARLES DE VALOIS, DUC D'ANGOULÊME, WHO RULED UNDER THE PROTECTION OF CARDINALS RICHELIEU AND MAZARIN, BOTH OF WHOM WIELDED MUCH POWER IN SEVENTEENTH-CENTURY FRANCE. THIS PORTRAIT OF MAZARIN DATES FROM 1840.

Valois, Duc d'Angoulême. Imprisoned in 1605 for conspiring against Henri IV, he was subsequently restored to favour and power in Angoulême under the protection of Cardinals Richelieu and Mazarin. The inclusion may be not so much prophetic as political, perhaps an adulteration by supporters of Richelieu and Mazarin. It is generally recognized that, in 1649, opponents who believed their influence in the French court was too great, planted *quatrains* angled against the Cardinal in an edition of the Prophecies on which the date had been forged as 1568, and it is reasonable to assume that the opposing faction might have resorted to similar measures.

The inclusion of the reference to Mars in the *quatrain*

has often been cited in support of the doomsday argument yet it draws on astrological lore selectively. Aggressive or brutal traits are only one aspect of Mars. In its more positive colours it is associated with love of freedom, strong leadership in crisis, decisiveness, defence of the weak, and sexual drive – not qualities readily associated with apocalypse.

In support of their apocalyptic scenario, authors tend to cite a significant passage in the letter to César in which Nostradamus describes *an abundance of fire and fiery missiles falling from the heavens so that nothing shall escape the holocaust. And this will occur before the last conflagration. For before war ends the century and its final stages, it will hold the century under its sway.* Nowhere in this context, however, does Nostradamus indicate which century he is describing, yet authors coolly link the content of the letter with **Q72 (CX)**, drawing the conclusion that the 'last conflagration' will take place in 1999 and that 'the century' means the twentieth century. It is wholly overlooked that a few sentences earlier in the same letter, Nostradamus refers to his work comprising prophecies 'from today until the year 3797'.

So what is the more logical interpretation of the *quatrain*?

For Nostradamus the term 'coming from the skies' would have had no meaning in the sense of airborne troops parachuting in, far less nuclear missiles raining down. On the other hand, it has already become increasingly apparent that Nostradamus placed not a little importance on the significance of comets as portents of major events in the world.

Response to unusual events of any kind in the skies was not limited to the medieval period. They had always been regarded as prophetic and were watched for carefully since long before the Christian era. In specifically Christian terms, the appearance of a bright star in the heavens indicated the coming of the Messiah and King, and modern biblical interpreters now generally regard this emanation as having been a comet.

The year 1997 witnessed the arrival of an unusually prominent comet, Hale-Bopp, clearly visible as a dramatic spectacle over the skies of France. The same year also saw the increasing political influence of the far right in France, particularly in the south of the country, perhaps presaging a new and virile leadership, a 'king' who will take power in 1999 as a cohesive focus riding in on a tide of nationalism. This equivalent of 'revival of the monarchy' may well take place both as a reaction against the burgeoning domination of Europe by Germany and after successive French governments have collapsed in the face of ongoing strikes and riots. These will be brought about by the social reforms imposed to reduce France's crippling social security burden and to achieve EU monetary union. It should not be forgotten that Le Pen, one of the most influential right-wing nationalist leaders of the 1990s, has established his power base in southern France, drawing on a deep well of antagonism against such issues as French

immigration policy. At the same time the increasingly unpopular Jacques Delors has found himself pelted with rotten eggs and custard pies.

Q72 (CI), however, suggests that at some time in the near future the adherents of extreme right-wing politics in France's political south will suffer retribution and be scattered. The prospect of almost a million dead or captive is either wildly inaccurate or suggests a forthcoming catastrophe on a far larger scale including, perhaps, the dire possibility of a nuclear catastrophe or an invasion of southern France from north Africa.

Du tout Marseille des inhabitants changée
Course & poursuitte jusqu'au près de Lyon,
Narbon, Tholoze par Bourdeaux outragée,
Tuez, captifs presque d'un million.

The people of Marseille are all changed, fleeing and pursued almost to Lyon. Narbonne and Toulouse outraged by Bordeaux, killed and taken prisoner nearly a million.

Whether the people of Marseilles are changed in their political colours or in some other way is unclear but the fact that they migrate en masse towards Lyon is indicative of an incident of not inconsiderable magnitude taking place at or near Marseilles.

Another *quatrain* in the 72 series which proves obscure is that of **Q72 (CII)**:

Armée Celtique en Italie vexée,
De toutes pars conflict & grande perte:
Romains fuis, o Gaule repoulsée,
Pres de Thesin, Rubicon pugne incerte.

Celtic army troubled in Italy, on all sides conflict and great loss. Romans flee, O Gaul repulsed. Near to Thesin, the battle of the Rubicon uncertain.

If we treat this *quatrain* literally it makes poor sense, but if we disregard individual place names and assume it to be an allegory it becomes more intelligible. It then describes a conflict between Roman Catholics, represented by 'Italy', and opposing forces represented, in the non-secular

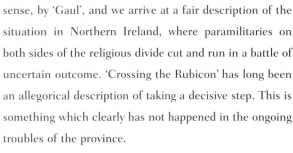

sense, by 'Gaul', and we arrive at a fair description of the situation in Northern Ireland, where paramilitaries on both sides of the religious divide cut and run in a battle of uncertain outcome. 'Crossing the Rubicon' has long been an allegorical description of taking a decisive step. This is something which clearly has not happened in the ongoing troubles of the province.

Q72 (CVIII), on the other hand, appears to indicate a more decisive battle in which the Catholic forces are put down. Again we are looking at allegory based on Nostradamus' own experience and the *quatrain* may refer to the Northern Ireland hostilities, supporting the predictions of *Q72 (CII)*. Perugia and Ravenna were both Papal States until the conquest by Gaston de Foix at Ravenna in 1512.

> *Champ Perusin o l'enorme deffaite*
> *Et le conflit tout au près de Ravenne,*
> *Passage sacre lors qu'on fera la feste*
> *Vainqueur vaincu cheval manger la venne.*

> *Oh, what great defeat on the field of Perugia, and the conflict very close to Ravenna. A holy passage when they will make the feast, the vanquished himself vanquished to eat horse meat.*

Even in this *quatrain*, despite its initial sense of victory, Nostradamus alludes to the fact that the winning side in the conflict will not remain victors for long.

The fact that it is reasonable to draw a non-apocalyptic interpretation of *Q72 (CX)* opens up a whole new scenario. Having established that it does not necessarily signal the beginning of the end in July 1999, but rather a radical if less dramatic change in the political coloration of the map of Europe, it also provides a firm starting point for assembling the rest of the jigsaw of pieces predicting events through into the twenty-first century.

THE COMET HALE-BOPP PHOTOGRAPHED IN MARCH 1997 IN ARIZONA, USA: BOTH ITS GAS AND DUST TAILS CAN BE SEEN. THE GAS TAIL IS BLUE AND IS BLOWN AWAY FROM THE COMET HEAD BY THE SOLAR WIND. THE WHITE DUST TAIL IS PUSHED AWAY FROM THE HEAD BY THE RADIATION OF SUNLIGHT.

JUST AS THERE IS AN AMUSING GAME TO BE PLAYED BY DRAWING ON PROPHECIES AT RANDOM and applying them to historical events which sound vaguely appropriate, so there is a comparable exercise in letting the imagination run riot and interpreting the quatrains of Nostradamus which seem to predict our future in the twenty-first century more or less as fancy takes us.

the NEXT THOUSAND YEARS

i n the past, the whimsies of Nostradamus-watchers have been driven by the fashionable imagery of the day and, so, whilst the cold war was in full spate, the astrological 'map' of our future generally included a nuclear holocaust triggered by the Soviet Union. Nowadays it has become popular to envisage catastrophe coming in the form of Islamic or Chinese expansionism, or possibly a combination of both.

It is possible, however, to make a more mature assessment of Nostradamus' predictions from the *quatrain* 72 series onwards, based on what we already know of his techniques, and on the most probable ways in which the world we live in is likely to change. It does not imply that we can assume Nostradamus to have anticipated all of the major events which may come about in future centuries, since it is clear from the *quatrains* already examined that he has tended to focus regularly on military and strategic matters whilst throwing in other predictions

AN ARTWORK IMPRESSION OF AN ASTEROID APPROACHING THE EARTH ABOUT 65 MILLION YEARS AGO: THE IMPACT WOULD HAVE CAUSED DECADES OF LOW GLOBAL TEMPERATURES AND PROBABLY LED TO THE EXTINCTION OF THE DINOSAURS.

more intermittently. Nor can we automatically take the predictions at face value. It will still be necessary to decipher, on occasions, when his vocabulary is rendered inadequate for the task and he resorts to allegory.

What do we know of likely future adjustments to our world? Armed aggression, in one form or another, year by year, seems to be a well-proven aspect of the human make-up and, in respect of warfare, Nostradamus probably made a shrewd choice of subject matter on which to concentrate his prophetic abilities. The choice was not unlike that of the fairground palm-reader who tells us that we will meet a dark stranger or embark on a long journey since both offer a margin of safety on the part of the fortune-teller! Despite today's climate of political and social correctness we are, by nature, competitive and acquisitive animals and we have a tendency to settle our competitive urges, and our apparent need for self-gain, by fighting it out.

THE DELIBERATE DESTRUCTION OF KUWAIT'S OIL WELLS DURING THE GULF WAR OF 1991 DID NOTHING TO CONSERVE THE WORLD'S DIMINISHING SUPPLIES OF FOSSIL FUELS. THIS IS JUST ONE OF THE 360 OIL WELLS OF THE AL BURGAN FIELD THAT WERE SET ABLAZE.

It would seem, at the moment, that the most likely cause of armed unrest during the forthcoming decades will rest with Islamic fundamentalism, internecine strife amongst third-world countries, particularly those of central and southern Africa, the necessity to guard dwindling supplies of fossil fuels in the Middle East and, least likely, possible military adventures by an emergent superpower such as communist China.

We can be fairly certain that wars of the future, at least between more technologically advanced protagonists, will be fought with great precision using 'smart' weapons which will be concentrated on military personnel, equipment and installations, both offensive and defensive, to the exclusion of large sections of the civilian population. It has been pointed out that this will represent a return to the wars of the past in which civilian populations were hardly involved and matters were settled on remote fields of battle. It is equally clear that, in less technologically advanced societies, such as those in Africa, civilian populations will continue to suffer from the style

RWANDAN REFUGEES CROSSING RUZIZI BRIDGE INTO ZAIRE: THE PERSECUTION OF DEFENCELESS PEOPLE SEEMS UNLIKELY TO ABATE IN THE FORESEEABLE FUTURE.

of atrocity that characterized the Algerian terrorist campaign of the late 1990s. Terrorism and guerrilla warfare show no sign of abating and there appears little that authorities can do to combat their threat against defenceless people.

The distinct possibility also arises of mass destruction of life through two particularly unpleasant agencies. The stockpile of the old Soviet nuclear arsenal is poorly guarded, some of it in perilous condition, and evidence accumulates that weapons have been, and may continue to be, sold to those who have the cash to acquire them irrespective of the security or sanity of the purchasers. In addition we live with the grim reality that several Middle Eastern countries, including Iraq and Iran, have the capability to produce and deliver nuclear, chemical and biological weapons of mass destruction in the foreseeable future, if not today.

In terms of pure politics various nations, mostly concentrated in the Middle East, are now faced with the stark choice between democracy and ideological fundamentalism. If they take the latter course, as seems likely, they will be drawn into ever deeper introspection and will fall further behind the developed world with inevitable consequences for all of us. Whether such countries as Algeria and Libya, ominously close to the soft

underbelly of Europe, succumb to the policies of militant extremism and prepare to advance northwards is impossible to predict but it must remain a distinct possibility. It is worthy of note that, in 1997, Abu el Mundhir, the leader of the Algerian fundamentalist group, gave a television interview in which he articulated the view that 'all those hostile to Islam or who remain neutral – men, women and children – must all be killed'.

GUERRILLA WARFARE AND ARMED UNREST SEEM DESTINED TO CONTINUE AS VARIOUS FACTIONS PURSUE THEIR POLITICAL AIMS.

We may see changing patterns of disease emerging as we enter the twenty-first century. The next equivalent of the AIDS virus may not be mercifully limited to transmission through body fluids. It may be carried in airborne droplets, in which case the scenario becomes truly nightmarish. Elsewhere in medicine it is an accepted reality that our current stock of antibiotics is on the verge of retreat in the battle against super-bugs that have found ways of mutating and so developing immunity to penicillin and its derivatives.

One may be tempted to believe that traditional religion will disappear during the twenty-first century but this would be a failure to understand the basic human need for a sense of spirituality, which overcomes anything and everything that technology offers us by way of 'big bangs' and scientific evidence that 'death is final'. In spite of the decline in church-going in many parts of Europe, Roman Catholicism shows no sign of lessening in popularity, Bible-belt religion attracts expanding congregations in America and eastern philosophies are

gaining ground in many parts of the western world, whilst the fervour and passions of Islamic fundamentalism speak for themselves.

Perhaps the subject which has captured most attention from the media in recent years is the growing evidence of climatic change. Yet, standing back from the more lurid aspects, the effect of greenhouse gases on global warming may be inconsequential when set beside the changes in climate which have occurred naturally in the past and which are destined, in all probability, to occur again. The small rises in temperature which are currently providing so much of a talking point amongst scientists and governments may, in fact, be attributable more to other, long-term causes than emissions of carbon dioxide from our industrial machinery.

What, therefore, does Nostradamus have to offer in terms of these and other realities? We are given to understand that his series of predictions closes in the year 3797. If quatrain 100 represents that futuristic date whilst *quatrain* 72 refers to approximately the year 2000, simple

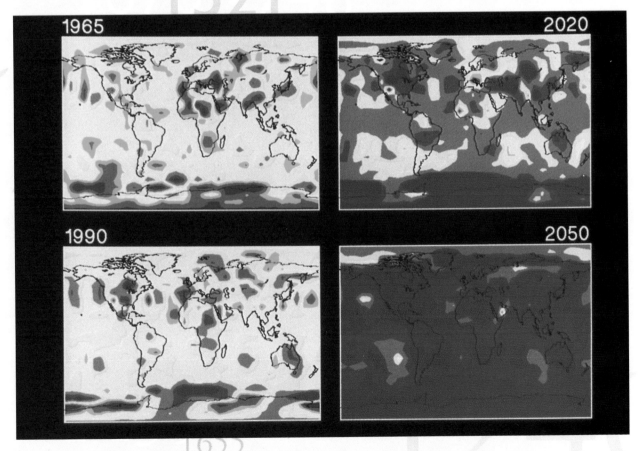

A SCIENTIFIC VIEW OF GLOBAL WARMING: COMPUTER-GENERATED IMAGES OF THE WORLD SHOW THE PROJECTED INCREASE IN SURFACE AIR TEMPERATURE TO THE YEAR 2050. RED AND ORANGE INDICATE INCREASED TEMPERATURES.

subtraction reveals an interval between each of the 28 *quatrains* of between 60 and 65 years. In other words, each *quatrain* now covers a period almost exactly ten times that reflected in the *quatrains* prior to the 72 series.

The *quatrain* 73 series, therefore, may be taken to cover at least the first half of the twenty-first century. *Q*73 (**CI**) possesses a strong ring of probability:

> *France à cinq pars par neglect assaillie,*
> *Tunys, Argel esmeuz par Persiens:*
> *Léon, Seville, Barcelonne faillie*
> *N'aura la classe par les Venetians.*

> *France assaulted by five countries through neglect. Tunis, Algiers stirred up by the Persians {Iranians}. Leon, Seville and Barcelona failed. They will not have the fleet because of the Venetians.*

The prediction suggests that France will be invaded, either through terrorism or direct assault, by five states and the clear indication is that these will be Islamic countries. We are given the names of two – Tunisia, Algeria – whose actions will be masterminded by a third, Iran. The others, predictably, are Morocco and, possibly, Iraq. To understand the significance of the reference to the Venetians and the absence of a protective naval fleet, one has to look back into an earlier period of history and to understand that Nostradamus was probably allegorizing.

During the fifteenth century Venice had risen to the peak of her power, gaining extensive possessions and building a powerful naval fleet. Historically the Venetian lagoon had served as a major trading focus between east and west and the Venetian men-of-war protected merchant convoys moving through the Mediterranean. By the 1500s the Venetian Empire still controlled significant parts of southern Europe, including Corfu, Crete, Cyprus, Negroponte and much of the coastline of the Balkans from Venice down as far as Durazzo. In the eyes of Nostradamus, 'Venetians' may have been a convenient term with which to identify a future Mediterranean peace-

THE SEMI-DESERT LANDSCAPE OF NORTH AFRICA TYPIFIES THE PARTS OF THE WORLD FROM WHICH NOSTRADAMUS ANTICIPATED MASS MOVEMENTS OF PEOPLE.

IN THE BATTLE OF LEPANTO IN 1571 THE FLEETS OF VENICE, SPAIN AND THE VATICAN DEFEATED THE TURKS. THE VENETIAN FLEET HAD BECOME ALMOST INVINCIBLE DURING THE FIFTEENTH AND SIXTEENTH CENTURIES AND ITS NAME WAS SYNONYMOUS WITH POWER.

keeping force that would fail to intercede to curb a military adventure out of north Africa, resulting in the overthrow of parts of Spain and an assault on southern France.

Some of the *quatrains* describing our future offer so little detail that they are of scant value, perhaps until after the event. They may turn out to be entirely accurate but only in hindsight. **Q73 (CIII)** provides a not untypical example:

Quand dans le regne parviendra le boiteux,
Competiteur aura proche bastard:
Luy & le regne viendront si fort roigneux,
Qu'ains qu'il guerisse son faict sera bien tard.

When the limping man reaches the kingdom, his rival
will be a bastard close to him. He and the kingdom will
become strongly cut back, so that the recovery he makes
will be too late.

How many kingdoms will exist in Europe in the twenty-first century? Perhaps only Great Britain, Belgium, some Scandinavian states and a scattering of princedoms and duchies. Or is the reference merely an allegory for a nation state which becomes controlled by a crippled leader and whose authority is contested by an illegitimate claimant?

Is that claimant's legitimacy negated by birth or by reason of other unsuitable credentials? All we know for certain is that the country will undergo a marked decline in consequence of this unhealthy rivalry and that the protagonists will awaken to the damage they are causing when it is too late for recovery.

One is tempted to seek a link between this *quatrain* and that of **Q73 (CIV)**:

Le nepueu grand par forces prouvera,
Le pache fait du coeur pusillanime:
Ferrare & Ast le Duc esprouvera,
Par lors qu'au soir sera le pantomime.

The nephew will be proved great by force of arms. The
crime is committed through faint-heartedness. The Duke
will put Ferrara and Asti to the test, then during the
evening the mime will take place.

A similar conflict amongst close relatives is hinted at here, a nephew winning the day over a cowardly uncle. Ferrara and Asti are towns in northern Italy but, in the modern context, they probably allegorize some other situation. It is interesting that in the fifteenth century, between 1438 and 1445, the last serious attempt was made by the Council of

Ferrara-Florence to resolve the split between eastern and western Christian Churches. One wonders, therefore, if the *quatrain* predicts an ideological dispute which splits a country and which involves a ruling family wrangle.

Q73 (CVIII) also seems to be focused on the same strategic situation as that of **Q73 (CI)** since, historically, the term 'Barbare' refers to piratical elements stemming from Algeria.

> *Soldat Barbare le grand Roy frappera*
> *Injustement non eslongne de mort,*
> *L'avare mere du fait cause sera*
> *Conivrateur & regne en grand remort.*

> *The Barbar soldier will strike the king unjustly, not far from death. The avaricious mother{land} will be the cause of the deed, conspirator and country in great remorse.*

The prophecy suggests that an inexcusable deed will be perpetrated against the leader of the invaded country which, from the *quatrains* already discussed, seems to be France but that this action will also bring about the downfall and lasting regret of the aggressor.

Another significant prophecy in the 73 series must be **Q73 (CX)** which predicts the rise of a great new world leader in the early part of the twenty-first century whose words of wisdom will be heeded too late.

> *The temps present avecques le passé*
> *Sera jugé par grand Jovialiste,*
> *Le monde tard luy sera lassé*
> *Et desloial par le clergé jouriste.*

> *The present time, together with the past will be judged by a great man of Jupiter. The world will tire of him too late, disloyal by the clerical jurors.*

The sense is somewhat obscure but the 'great man of Jupiter' has to be a world leader endowed with power and authority. It seems that the religious establishment, of whatever faith, will oppose him.

Of the remaining *quatrains* in the 73 series which cover our immediate future, that included in Century II

LAKE GARDA IN NORTHERN ITALY HAS BEEN PROPOSED AS THE LIKELY INTERPRETATION OF NOSTRADAMUS' REFERENCE TO BENAC.

seems particularly obscure yet clearly it has a specific, albeit hidden, meaning.

> *Au lac Fucin de Benac le rivaige*
> *Prins du Leman au port de l'Orguion:*
> *Nay de trois bras predict bellique image,*
> *Par trois couronnes au grand Endymion.*

> *From the shore of Lake Benac {allegedly Lake Garda in Italy} to Lake Fucino, taken from Leman {Geneva} to the port of Orguion: born of three arms it predicts a warlike image, through three kingdoms, to the great Endymion.*

It would appear that Nostradamus is predicting that a triple alliance of states will arise somewhere in Europe, though not necessarily Italy or Switzerland, since the place names he relies on have to be read as representatives familiar to him rather than, necessarily, the actual locations involved during the twenty-first century. We are given the number *three* twice in the *quatrain*. The only other obvious possibilities are that the *trois couronnes* refers obliquely to the three crowns in the heraldic symbolism of the Vatican or to the three stars in the make-up of the national flag of Iraq. We are also provided with the somewhat unusual place name Orguion of which there is no existing counterpart, nor is one known from history. The nearest we can come is to either Organya in Spain, the small town of Organ in southern France, or to Oregon in the United States. Portland, Oregon, lies on a river and therefore has to be a serious contender particularly since many observers decipher Endymion as a reference to the USA, sometimes accused in the past of being isolationist and the 'sleeping giant' in world affairs. One is tempted to look ahead to a Balkan alliance, or one headed by Iraq, which will present a military challenge to the American superpower in the early years of the next century. Either scenario presents a distinct possibility.

Q73 (CVI) is no less easy to address:

En cité grande un moyne & artisan,
Près de la porte logés & aux murailles:
Contre Modene secret, cave disant,
Trahis pour faire souz coleur d'espousailles

In a great city a monk and an artisan are lodged near
the gate and beside the walls: they speak secretly from
their hiding place, against Modena, betrayed for acting
under the guise of marriage.

Modena is an industrial town in northern Italy which was ruled, during Nostradamus' time, by the influential Este family dynasty. It possesses a Romanesque cathedral but otherwise offers no substantive clues. The only hint is that a cleric of some seniority, perhaps the pontiff, and a leader from the secular world, are destined to hatch some kind of plot whilst allied in an unholy marriage of convenience.

The equivalent *quatrain* in the series arising in Century IX is more interesting. Q73 (CIX) indicates that someone, clearly identified by his dress as an Islamic leader, will adopt a position of influence for a period of time and will then disappear into obscurity.

Dans Fois entrez Roy ceiulée turbao,
Et regnera moins revolu Saturne
Roy Turban blanc Bizance couer ban,
Sol, Mars, Mercure près la hurne.

In time a blue-turbaned king enters and will reign for
less than a cycle of Saturn. A white-turbaned king will
be exiled to Byzantium {the east}. Sun, Mars, Mercury near
to Aquarius.

Elsewhere in the *Centuries*, Nostradamus also refers to the 'white' being succeeded by the 'blue' and the white turban is a characteristic garb of the Ayatollahs in Iran. It appears that the influence of the leader will, however, be comparatively short-lived. A single cycle of Saturn takes up slightly less than thirty years. The astrological part of the prediction offers little clue to the dating and the word *Fois* is vague, perhaps referring to the time when the blue-turbaned king makes his debut.

Moving ahead to the next 60-year predictive span, Q74 (CX) contains one of the most grim of Nostradamus' prophecies and it indicates that sometime during the latter half of the twenty-first century the final number, the

ALBRECHT DURER'S PORTRAYAL OF THE VISION DESCRIBED IN
THE BOOK OF REVELATION IN WHICH GOD HANDS TRUMPETS
TO SEVEN ANGELS: THE SOUNDS OF THE TRUMPETS HERALD THE
ONSET OF DISASTERS TO BE VISITED UPON THE EARTH, IN
PREPARATION FOR THE SECOND COMING.

'Seventh Seal' described in the *Book of Revelation*, will be opened, thus paving the way for the 'age of the great millennium'. This prophecy would seem to indicate that the millennium build-up, which Nostradamus believed would begin in the eighteenth century, will not necessarily be drawing to a close by the twenty-first century, but its building blocks will all be in place and there will be nothing to impede the Second Coming when the dead will arise.

Au revolu du grand nombre septiesme
Apparoistra au temps jeux d'Hacatombe,
Non esloigné du grand eage milliesme
Que les entres sortiront de leur tombe.

At the turning of the great seventh number, it will appear at the time of the games of great public sacrifice. Not far from the great age of the millennium when the dead will leave their tombs.

In this *quatrain* Nostradamus seems to be suggesting that there will take place not necessarily some all-engulfing apocalyptic battle but that there will be a loss of life on a major scale. This may equate with the description of the activities of the seven angels in Revelation 8, which include the delivery of thunder, lightning, earthquakes, volcanic eruptions and, most significantly, a comet impacting with the earth. Many palaeontologists now believe that it was the collision between our planet and a large extraterrestrial body which caused the extinction of the dinosaurs millions of years ago, and astronomers concede that a similar catastrophe, the impact of some nemesis asteroid, is likely to happen again in the future. Such a possibility has come closer with the recent discovery of an asteroid that could collide with the earth in 2028.

Q74 (CII) offers a more specific forecast and suggests a movement from France across the Pyrenees and another taking place in Italy, although the wording is somewhat confused:

De Sens, d'Autun viendront jusques au Rosne
Pour passer outre vers les monts Pyrenées:
La gent sortir de la Marque d'Anconne,
Par terre & mer suivra à grans trainées.

From Sens, from Autun they will come as far as the Rhone, to pass over towards the Pyrenees. The populace leaves the Marches of Ancona By land and sea they follow in great convoys.

The geography of this *quatrain* seems thoroughly muddled. Sens and Autun lie in north-east France, whilst the Rhone valley would take them into the south-east around Lyon. The Marches of Ancona lie in Italy. Disregarding the sequence of words it is possible, however, to discern a message. There will be a general exodus of population in both France and Italy and the movement will pass either south or north, though the direction is unclear. As to why this migration will take place there is also no clue.

Another *quatrain* in the 74 series, however, may provide answers. **Q74 (CV)** reads:

De sang Troyen naistra coeur Germanique
Qu'il deviendra en si haute puissance:
Hors chassera gent estrange Arabique
Tournant l'Eglise en pristine préeminence.

Of Trojan blood will be born a German heart who will become a very powerful man. He will chase away the Arabic foreigners and turn the Church back to its pristine glory.

GUARDIANS OF THE FRONTIER BETWEEN FRANCE AND SPAIN, THE PYRENEES HAVE NEVERTHELESS PERMITTED ACCESS THROUGH THEIR HIGH PASSES FOR MIGRATION AT VARIOUS KEY POINTS IN HISTORY

Le deschassée au regne tournera

Ses ennemis trouvés des conjures:

Plus que jamais son temps triomphera

Trois & septante à mort trop asseures.

The dethroned woman will return to her reign, her enemies found amongst the conspirators. More than ever she will rule triumphantly, at seventy-three she will assuredly die.

This *quatrain* clearly suggests a strategic situation whereby Muslim immigrants, whether they have previously arrived by peaceful means or aggressive invasion, are driven out of Europe through the influence of a single figure. Consequently the Christian Church, which has been censured in favour of Islam, is returned to its former position of authority. As to whom the Trojan-blooded German might be we are given no indication, although it is suggested by Erika Cheetham that the term 'Trojan' is used by Nostradamus for one of French royal extraction. In today's terms that might be interpreted as a leader from the extreme political right. The *quatrain* suggests that there will be a major reaction against Muslim fundamentalism in Europe and this now begins to explain the migration of people from Italy and from France, south by way of the Pyrenees, that is described in Century II though without a clear direction of movement.

Q74 (CVI) offers an interesting future view of the monarchy, or conceivably, of a presidential leader. In either event, it refers to a woman who experiences diverse fortunes:

We are looking ahead into the second half of the twenty-first century so it is possible that the individual referred to in the *quatrain* has not yet been born. She could, however, be living today, aged no more than 20 or 25 years. There is no indication of where in the world she will reign. The obvious monarchy is, of course, that of Great Britain, but no future queen is evident in the existing royal family. From the description of her fall and rise the prophecy is unlikely to be referring anachronistically to Queen Elizabeth II. Other possibilities are the Presidency of the United States which, to date, has never been voted to a woman but America is a country in which women are

THE NEW LAND REFERRED TO IN THE PROPHECIES SUGGESTS THE MODERN SUPERPOWER OF THE UNITED STATES, SYMBOLIZED HERE BY THE FAMILIAR IMAGE OF THE WHITE HOUSE.

SONIA GANDHI, WIDOW OF RAJIV GANDHI, HAS ENTERED THE POLITICAL ARENA, FOLLOWING IN THE FOOTSTEPS OF OTHER WOMEN LEADERS IN THE SECOND HALF OF THE TWENTIETH CENTURY. CONTINUING THIS TREND, A POWERFUL FEMALE RULER IS PREDICTED TO BECOME PROMINENT IN THE LATER TWENTY-FIRST CENTURY.

already taking ever more significant roles in politics. It should be noted that the prophecy does not state that she will *rule* for 73 years, only that she will live for that length of time. As the twentieth century draws to a close we have also witnessed highly influential women in power in such states as Israel, India and Pakistan. Clearly this woman will not have an easy time and will be 'dethroned' for a while before making her come-back.

It is tempting to play games in this series of *quatrains* by linking **CVI** and **CVIII** which also refers to a situation involving the monarchy.

> *En terre neufue bien avant Roy entré*
> *Pendant subges luy viendront faire acueil,*
> *Sa perfidie aura tel recontré*
> *Qu'aux citadins lieu de feste & recueil.*

The translation of this *quatrain* is difficult and, to an extent, it must be paraphrased. *Whilst well before the king enters a new land subjects will come to make him welcome, his treachery will have met with such [opprobrium] that, to the citizen he will be received rather than feted.*

The indication here is that a leader-in-opposition has received considerable support from his own backers but that his duplicity makes him generally unpopular when he finally takes office. This, in turn, suggests that the person will not rule for very long. It may be, therefore, that he represents the short-term intrusion into the more lasting popularity of the woman leader. The *quatrain* also adds to the possibility, if the two prophecies are linked, that the location of **Q74** (**CVI**) is indeed the United States because the term *terre neufue* was in popular usage in Nostradamus' day to describe the newly discovered lands of the Americas.

A fascinating observation on a reversion to paganism is to be found in *Q74 (CIX)*.

Dans la cité de Fertsod homicide,
Fait & fait multe beuf arant ne macter,
Retour encores aux honneurs d'Artemide
Et à Vulcan corps morts sepulturer.

In the city of Fertsod {there is} killing, again and again many oxen go {to plough?} but not to slaughter. A return once more to the honours of Artemis, and to Vulcan the corpses of the dead to bury.

GERMAN TROOPS ENTERING PRAGUE IN 1939: THERE IS EVIDENCE THAT ONE OF HITLER'S AMBITIONS WAS TO REINSTATE CERTAIN NORDIC PAGAN PRACTICES, AND A REVIVAL OF INTEREST IN PAGAN IDEOLOGY CANNOT BE RULED OUT IN THE FUTURE.

Although the city of Fertsod cannot be placed with any certainty, and although Roman deities are listed, the location of this prophecy is clearly Scandinavia and the city referred to could be the town of Farsø in Jutland. The practice of ceremonial or ritual ploughing by oxen was practised widely in pre-Christian times in Norway and Denmark to create sacred fields. It was also a time-honoured Norse rite to cremate the dead on great funeral pyres, a ceremony which was featured more recently in Wagner's operatic *Ring Cycle*. Vulcan was a god of fire.

The implication of the prophecy is that parts of Scandinavia, a region which was one of the last to abandon paganism in favour of Christianity, will dispense with the Christian Church and revert to the worship of the old Norse gods, the Aesir and Vanir pantheons. This is not quite as far-fetched as it may appear on first reading. One of Adolf Hitler's underlying ambitions, should the Third Reich have succeeded in triumphing over the allied forces in the Second World War, was to reinstate the rites of the god Odin and his ancient Nordic pantheon with its warrior maidens, its runic lore and its mythical castle of Valhalla. On the walls of the Reich Chancellor's bunker in Berlin Hitler demonstrated his obsession to the extent of having artists depict his storm troopers equipped with wings and horned helmets protecting the pure Aryan youth upon which he set so much store for the future. The evidence of this neo-pagan ideology has been discovered recently and it is possible that such a movement will arise again at some time in the future.

Amongst the most terrifying of Nostradamus' prophecies is one which is detected in the obscure lines of **Q75 (CII)**. It is perhaps the awesome prediction of our children's future.

> *La voix ouye de l'insolit oyseau*
> *Sur le canon du respiral estage:*
> *Si hault viendra du froment le boisseau*
> *Que l'homme d'homme sera Antropophage.*

Various Nostradamus-watchers have made the mistake of neglecting the literal translation of this *quatrain* and have looked for metaphors amongst its curious wording. Yet the prophecy needs no paraphrasing and its meaning is the literal one. Its warning is one which we receive stridently, day by day, but choose to ignore.

> *The call of the strange bird is heard on the pipe of the*
> *breathing floor: so high will become the bushels of wheat*
> *that man will cannibalise his fellow man.*

It is not the *quantity* of wheat that will rise so high but the *cost*. The strange bird is the bird of death, the vulture, and the 'pipe of the breathing floor' is the chilling phrase which Nostradamus uses to describe the earth's lungs, starved of oxygen and water, to the extent that crops no longer grow and man recourses to eating man.

Recently, in the remote Australian outback a single

remaining tribe of nomadic Aboriginals was located by an American anthropologist, Marlo Morgan, who lived with them for four months on walkabout and then wrote an account of her experience that is both shocking and deeply

LIVING IN CLOSE HARMONY WITH THE NATURAL WORLD, THE ABORIGINALS OF THE AUSTRALIAN OUTBACK ARE KEENLY AWARE OF THE EARTH'S VULNERABILITY IN THE FACE OF RELENTLESS CLIMATIC CHANGE.

THE DISTURBING SIGHT OF A DROUGHT-STRICKEN LANDSCAPE WILL BECOME INCREASINGLY FAMILIAR AS THE EARTH IS STARVED OF WATER AND OXYGEN.

moving. The very existence of the tribe is denied by the Australian government, yet it represents all that is left of the pure indigenous culture of the continent and its links with the natural world are amongst the closest to be found anywhere on the planet.

The tribe, which the author identifies only as the 'Real People', has adopted voluntary celibacy out of a reasoning that is both simple and dreadful. Their conviction is that the world in which they have the capacity to survive is dying. They recognize this as a certainty and they intend to die with it, to become extinct hand in hand with the womb which gave them life. Water is becoming impossible to find in the outback, radiation levels from the sun are rising and so too is the temperature. The animals and plants on which they have depended since time immemorial are disappearing so that they can no longer find adequate nourishment. Meanwhile the technologically advanced world pours scorn on this simple understanding that whatever we do to the web of life, we also do to ourselves. Perhaps they see clearly what we cannot, or rather do not wish, to see. The *quatrain* date takes us about 100–150 years into the future.

Of scarcely less concern is the *quatrain* in the same series from *Century* III. **Q75 (CIII)** depicts the arrival of a new plague amidst great conflict, although this epidemic is qualified in a curious manner.

Pau, Verone, Vicence, Sarragousse,
De glaives loings terroirs de sang humides:
Peste si grand viendra à la grand gousse,
Proche secours, & bien loing les remedes.

Pau, Verona, Vicenza, Saragossa, the swords of distant
lands wet with blood. A great pestilence will come in the
great husk. Help nearby but remedy far away.

We are offered a vision of major war in Europe, driven by forces from beyond the continent and with it will come disease carried in a husk or shell. This is a clear indication that biological warfare will erupt at some time during the twenty-second century and that some infection, such as bubonic plague or anthrax, will be carried in a missile. The possibility of this catastrophe occurring is a very real one. Since the time of the Gulf War with Iraq, one of the most pressing concerns of the United Nations has been to seek out and destroy that country's weapons of mass destruction. It is recognized that both Iraq and Iran have

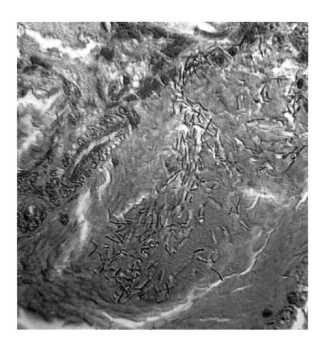

THE DEADLY ANTHRAX BACTERIUM SEEN IN TISSUE AT A
MAGNIFICATION OF 33.

the capacity to manufacture biological weapons and both are considered to possess the technical expertise, if not the immediate means, to deliver them by medium-range missile into the Mediterranean regions of Europe.

In *Q75* (*CIX*) we find a possible amplification on the perilous situation described in the Century III *quatrain*:

Del l'Ambraxie & du pays de Thrace,
Peuple par mer mal & secours Gaulois,
Perpetuelle en Provence la trace,
Avec vestiges de leur coustume & loix.

From Arta and the country of Thrace, people ill by sea
and French help. The evidence permanent in Provence,
with vestiges of their customs and laws.

The implication seems to be that the Mediterranean region will see an exodus of people who are ill or diseased and that these blighted emigrées will settle in southern France.

Moving forward in time to the *quatrain* 77 series, some 300 years ahead, one finds reference to an armed clash between Iran and Egypt, presumably over issues of Islamic fundamentalism under the pressures of which Egypt is already suffering. *Q77* (*CIII*) indicates that the Egyptian forces will find themselves on the winning side.

FUTURE EPIDEMICS OF PLAGUE MAY COME IN THE FORM OF
BIOLOGICAL WARFARE. WILL THE MILITARY GAS MASKS OF
TODAY, EQUIPPED WITH FILTERS TO ABSORB POISONOUS GASES,
BECOME EVERYDAY WEAR IN THE FUTURE?

TENSIONS ALREADY APPARENT IN EGYPT BETWEEN MODERATE AND FUNDAMENTALIST ISLAMIC IDEOLOGIES LOOK SET TO INCREASE.

Le tiers climat sous Aries comprins,
L'an mil sept cens vingt & sept en Octobre:
Le roy de Perse par caux d'Egypt prins:
Conflit, mort, perte à la croix grand opprobre.

The third climate included under Aries in October in the year 1727. The Persian king taken prisoner by the forces of Egypt: conflict, death, loss, great opprobrium to the cross.

According to the logic of this book the date included in the *quatrain* is one of those 'red herrings' designed to fool the reader into believing that Nostradamus jumbled up the sequence of the prophecies. It is a detail so glaringly introduced that its purpose should be obvious. Nostradamus is playing a game in which he requires us only to exercise a little research elsewhere in his *Centuries*. Comparison of this *quatrain* with **Q77 (CVIII)** produces some intriguing parallels.

L'antichrist troi bien tout annichilez,
Vingt & sept ans sang durera sa guerre,
Les heretiques morts, captifs, exilez,
Sang corps humain eau rogie gresler terre.

The third antichrist annihilates all thoroughly. Twenty-seven years of bloodshed will be endured in his war. Heretics dead, captive, exiled. Bloody human remains and red sand covering the ground.

The 'third climate' under the warlike Aries and the 'third antichrist' would appear to be one and the same. Yet there is also a similarity, too obvious to ignore, in the years mentioned in both *quatrains*. The first of the prophecies throws in a spurious year date unless one appreciates that its significance lies only in the last two numbers, 27, or that it includes two mutually exclusive numbers, because the second parallel *quatrain* also specifically refers to a period of 27 years. It seems that Nostradamus occasionally expects us to do a little lateral inspection of his predictions! Perhaps he is suggesting that the conflict will begin in the seventeenth year of the century in question and will last for 27 years. In about 2317 CE there will arise a protracted conflict between an essentially Christian Egypt and an Islamic Iran in which the Iranian forces will eventually be routed and their leader taken prisoner, whilst the desert sands are left covered in the blood of the war's victims. The conduct of the Christian forces, however, will be disgraceful and as a result they will bring the Church into considerable disrepute.

Two *quatrains* in the 78 series, which takes us further into the twenty-fourth century, seem pointedly to refer to an identical personality who will become a dangerously weak leader of France or Europe. **Q78 (CI)** describes an idiot, lacking in skills of intellect and warfare:

D'un chef vieillard naistra sens hebeté
Degenerant par savoir & par armes:
Le chef de France par sa soeur redouté,
Champs divisez, concedez aux gendarmes.

From an aged leader will be born a stupid one {literally of dazed senses}, degenerate both in knowledge and military strategy. The {new} leader of France will be dreaded by his sister. Camps will be divided and {authority} conceded to the army.

In other words, the political machinery will fail in consequence of a weak and deranged leader inheriting control, and power will of necessity be placed in the hands of the military authorities.

A not dissimilar forecast is provided in **Q78 (CII)** though the reference is less overt and easy to overlook:

Le grand Neptune du profond de la mer,
De gent Punique & sang Gaulois meslé:
Les Isles à sang pour le tardif ramer,
Plus luy nuira que l'occult mal celé.

Great Neptune from the depths of the sea, from people of
mixed French and north African blood. The islands
will be bloody because of the staying of the retarded one.
More harm to him than the badly concealed secret.

This prophecy amplifies upon the previous *quatrain*, suggesting that obstinacy in clinging to power by the idiot will result in bloodshed, but that his persistence will inevitably wreak a greater harm on himself than will the disclosure that he is mentally defective. An indication of where this conflict may be focused emerges in **Q77 (CI)**:

Entre deux mers dressera promontoire,
Que puis mourra pars le mords du cheval:
Le sien Neptune pliera voille noire,
Par Calpre & classe auprès de Rocheval.

Between two seas is sited a promontory where one will
die through a horse's bite. For his family Neptune will
furl the black flag. Between Calpre {Gibraltar} and
close by Rocheval lies the fleet.

GUSTAVE DORÉ'S ENGRAVING ILLUSTRATES THE FOURTH HORSEMAN, 'WHOSE NAME WAS DEATH', ENVISIONED BY THE WRITER OF APOCALYPSE.

The precise meaning is unclear but the reference to death from a horse's bite is perhaps an illustration of Nostradamus resorting to biblical quotation: *And I looked, and behold a pale horse: and his name that sat on him was Death.* (Revelation 6:8). The reference to Neptune, god of the sea, and the black flag of death also possesses a poetic

AS GOD OF THE SEA, NEPTUNE SYMBOLIZES THE POWER OF THE OCEAN, HIS NAME FREQUENTLY INVOKED IN ART AND LITERATURE. THIS PICTURE DECORATES A MUSIC SHEET OF C.1860.

Tous les degrez d'honneur Ecclesiastique,
Seront changez en dial quirinal:
En Martial quirinal flaminique,
Puis un Roy de France le rendre vulcanal.

All degrees of ecclesiastical honour will be changed into
Jupiter's 'quirinal'. The 'quirinal' will be in martial
guise, then a French leader will make it 'vulcanal'.

It is clear immediately that this prophecy is full of symbolism and metaphor and it is therefore not easy to decipher. The first two lines suggest that ecclesiastical authority will be taken over by the state. Quirinus was the Roman god of peaceful assembly or *quirinal*. He was one of a triad of deities with Jupiter and Mars, and Romans in their civil capacity became known as Quirites, whilst Mars presided over their more martial activities. The word *dial* which appears in the second line of the Old French is a corruption of Dyaus from which Deus or Zeus comes, and on that more ancient prototype the Roman god Jupiter was modelled. Vulcan has nothing overtly to do with this trio and stands as a rather unattractive Roman fire god who shunned the company of other deities and was himself fairly unpopular amongst his celestial peers. The second part of the prophecy indicates, therefore, that the state assembly will become somewhat aggressive, a French civic leader will render it thoroughly unpopular or 'vulcanal' with the populace and, presumably, power will be returned to the ecclesiastical authority.

There occurs a very distinct cluster of prophecies in and around the *quatrain* 85 series which together indicate a catastrophe on a more massive scale. Nostradamus either refers directly or alludes to this event in no less than eight *quatrains* distributed through at least five of the *Centuries* between series 84 and 86. The chronology takes us forward between 700 and 800 years into the future and the general thrust of the prophecies suggests that an occurrence which is being widely predicted by modern-day astronomers and geophysicists will take place in that period.

The initial indications come in the *quatrain* 84 series. **Q84 (CIII)** tells of a city shortly to be abandoned by its inhabitants:

flavour and is deeply rooted in mythology. On the assumption that Gibraltar has not left British sovereignty, the indication is that British, French and Spanish forces will be involved in an affray over territorial rights to the Rock.

Another fascinating, though not necessarily related, event is predicted to take place in the same time period of the early twenty-fourth century. It is described in **Q77 (CV)**:

NOSTRADAMUS' USE OF MARS AS A SYMBOL OF STRIFE AND AGGRESSION CONTRASTS WITH THE VERY LITERAL PORTRAYAL OF THE ROMAN GOD OF WAR IN THIS SEVENTEENTH-CENTURY ENGRAVING. AS HIS CHARIOT PASSES OVERHEAD, SOLDIERS STEAL CATTLE, BURN HOMES AND ATTEMPT TO KIDNAP A WOMAN AND HER CHILDREN.

La grand cité sera bien desolée
Des habitans un seul n'y demoura
Mur, sexe, temple, & vierge violée,
Par fer, feu, peste, cannon peuple mourra.

The great city will soon be totally deserted. Of its inhabitants not one will remain. City wall, members, church and virgin violated. People will die from the sword, fire, pestilence and gun.

We are offered a grim vision of a major metropolis somewhere in the world entering a state of panic, its citizens fleeing the city and their exodus accompanied by the inevitable break-down of law and order. There is looting, killing and rape. But why? What do they fear?

Q84 (CI) may provide part of the answer:

Lune obscurcie aux profondes ténèbres,
Son frère passe de couleur ferrugine
Le grand caché long temps soubs les ténèbres,
Tiedera fer dans la plaie sanguine.

The moon obscured in great darkness, her brother becoming coloured like blood. The great one hidden for a long time in the darkness will cast its iron blade into the bloody wound.

Nostradamus has foreseen the precise conditions resulting from either a nuclear strike or a meteoric impact from an extra-terrestrial source and, from his choice of words, the latter possibility seems more likely. The moon will be obscured by dust clouds, the sun will appear blood red. The comet or asteroid, for thousands of years hidden in the darkness of space, will rip through the atmosphere and collide with the earth with terrible effect. Scientists will, inevitably, have been charting the course of this celestial nemesis and will have urged evacuation of the region upon which the comet will strike.

In **Q84 (CV)** Nostradamus is again preoccupied with this apocalyptic event, though in more poetic terms.

Naistra du gouphre & cité immesurée,
Nay de parents obscurs & ténébreux:
Qui la puissance du grand roy reverée
Voudra destruire par Rouan & Eureux.

Born of the abyss and the immeasurable city, born of dark and obscure parents who wish to destroy the power of the revered king through Rouen and Europe.

We should perhaps ignore Rouen and take it that the word symbolizes only a great city. This is a catastrophe which is destined to touch all of Europe. The comet, born in the abyss of the cosmos out of some mysterious parentage, has been sent as divine retribution on a mission of destruction.

In **Q85 (CII)** Nostradamus describes this death-dealing body as it would have been perceived by his generation of observers:

THE GREAT BEAR AS PORTRAYED IN *URANIA'S MIRROR, OR A VIEW OF THE HEAVENS*, PUBLISHED ABOUT 1820: THIS CONSTELLATION WAS WELL KNOWN TO ASTROLOGERS IN THE MIDDLE AGES AND IS MENTIONED IN SOME OF THE PROPHECIES.

Le vieux plain barbe soubs le statut sévère,
A Lyon faict dessus l'Aigle Celtique:
Le petit grant trop outre persévère
Bruit d'arme au ciel: mer rouge Lygustique.

Under the severe authority of the old man with the white
beard, he is placed above the Celtic Eagle at Lyons. The
small great one perseveres too much; noise of celestial
weapons, the Ligurian sea red.

The old man with the white beard is the symbol of time and mortality whose authority is severe and greater than that of principalities. Meanwhile the comet, at first so tiny to the naked eye and yet so great a force, presses on through the vastness of the universe and reaches towards us with a great roaring in the sky. The sea turns red with its reflection.

In **Q85 (CVIII)** Nostradamus again refers to the blotting out of light and to an asphyxiating presence:

Entre Bayonne & à Saint Jean de Lux,
Sera posé de Mars la Promottoire
Aux Hanix d'Aquilon Nanar hostera lux
Puis suffocqué au lict sans adiutoire.

Between Bayonne and Saint Jean of the Light, the region
of Mars will be positioned. To Hanix of the north,
Nanar will capture the light, then {people} are
suffocated in {their} beds without help.

The *quatrain* refers to some obscure region of the northern hemisphere but the implication must be that a large tract of land will succumb to violence through something, or someone, referred to as Nanar. Tantalizingly, this may have come down to us as a misprint of the name Namar, or

ACCORDING TO NOSTRADAMUS, THE SUN WILL BE 'COLOURED LIKE BLOOD' – PERHAPS LOOKING AS IT DOES IN THIS STRIKING SILHOUETTE, CAPTURED BY SOLAR TELESCOPE, OF A MAN STANDING ON A MOUNTAIN RIDGE OVER SEVEN MILES AWAY.

Namtar, from which Nemesis derives. In very ancient times Namtar was a god of fate, whilst Nemesis was the Greek goddess of revenge and justice. Nostradamus envisages a vast suffocating dust cloud which blots out the sun.

Other *quatrains* seem to allude to the same happening. *Q85 (CIII)*, which follows that of *Q84 (CIII)* describing a city being deserted by its inhabitants, indicates that the city will be taken by trickery and deceit. To a superstitious-minded sixteenth-century writer such an event may well have been envisaged as a malevolent and underhanded caprice instigated by the powers of heaven. In *Q86 (CV)* one finds details of how the city will be inundated by the flooding of the river on which it is sited, its civic leaders scattered, wandering aimlessly. Flooding would be one of the inevitable short-term repercussions of a strike by a comet or an asteroid.

Some kind of natural disaster involving a serious disruption of the earth's surface is emphasized in another *quatrain* of the 86 series. *Q86 (CII)* combines this warning

with an indication of Islamic aggression, possibly by a fundamentalist regime against a more moderate Egypt:

Naufrage à classe pres d'onde Hadriatique,
La terre tremble esmeue sus l'air en terre mis:
Egypte tremble augment Mahometique,
L'Herault soy rendre à crier est commis.

A fleet is wrecked near the Adriatic, the earth trembles,
rises into the air and settles to the ground. Egypt trembles
against Mahommedan uprising. The herald is sent for to
ask for surrender.

The description of the earth trembling, rising into the air and falling again is very pertinent to what might happen in the event of a major cometary or asteroidal impact.

Away from this event, futuristic references to the plague re-emerge, after a long absence from the *quatrains*, in a contemporary period at *Q85 (CIV)*:

A SMALL STREAM HAS BECOME A TORRENT AFTER HEAVY RAIN HIGH IN THE ANDES OF ECUADOR. SUDDEN FLOODING LIKE THIS WOULD RESULT FROM A COMET OR AN ASTEROID COLLIDING WITH THE EARTH, A POSSIBILITY PREDICTED IN MORE THAN ONE *QUATRAIN*.

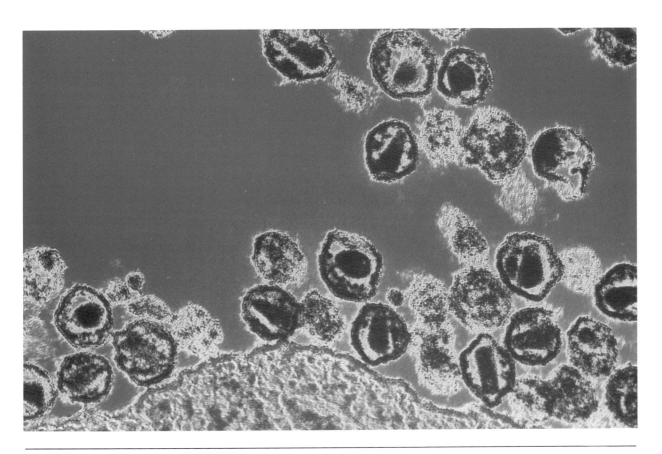

THIS COLOURED TRANSMISSION ELECTRON MICROGRAPH SHOWS A T-LYMPHOCYTE BLOOD CELL INFECTED WITH HIV, THE CAUSATIVE AGENT OF AIDS. THE T-CELL, SEEN AT THE BOTTOM, IS SURROUNDED BY VIRUS PARTICLES WHICH INFECT OTHER T-CELLS BY A PROCESS OF VIRAL BUDDING. AIDS-TYPE EPIDEMICS COULD POSE AN INCREASING THREAT TO HUMAN HEALTH IN THE FUTURE.

Le charbon blanc du noir fera chassé
Prisonnier faict mené au tombereau:
More chameau fus piedz entrelassez
Lors le puisné fillera l'aubereau

The white charbon is driven away by the black:
made a prisoner, led to the gallows. His feet are tied
together like a camel {criminal}, when the last born will
release the falcon.

Dans les cyclades, en perinthe & larisse
Dedans Sparte tout le Pelloponnesse:
Si grand famine, peste par faux connisse.
Neuf mois tiendra & tout le cherronesse.

In the Cyclades, in Perinthus and Larissa, in Sparta
and all of the Peloponnese, a great famine, plague
through false dust. It will last nine months throughout
all of the peninsula.

Since Nostradamus does not use the term *charbon* for the plague, the *quatrain* suggests that here he is referring to something wholly different. 'White carbon' could be ashes or even diamonds – most probably ashes, representing the old, giving way, amidst violence, to the dark coals of the new.

The next reference, in **Q90 (CV)**, which takes us even further ahead in time to the thirty-first century, is more interesting. It refers to *peste* rather than *charbon*, Nostradamus' more usual euphemism, though a pestilence that is delivered through a 'false dust':

The fact that this 'plague' is borne by means of a 'false dust' suggests strongly that Nostradamus anticipated some kind of lethal airborne substance being unleashed either in the form of a biological or chemical weapon, or through droplets of breath in an AIDS-type epidemic. In 1988 the world witnessed the use of chemical agents amongst the Turkish and Iraqi Kurds which killed large sections of civilian population. We have also seen the effectiveness of airborne defoliants in destroying crops and thereby inducing famine. Nostradamus is predicting

a similar future disaster to occur in Greece and the Balkans

Hard on the heels of *quatrain* 90, the third reference comes in *Q91 (CIX)* and clearly refers to the same catastrophe in the Greek peninsula and parts of Turkey where the modern equivalents of all its listed place names are to be found. But again it seems a carefully qualified statement because it describes an *unknown* evil, suggesting that this is not the same plague as that which Nostradamus recognizes in the sixteenth century. The words take on a chilling ring since we know that a number of countries already have the capacity to manufacture biological weapons, including those containing such lethal organisms as Anthrax.

L'horrible peste Perynte & Nicopolle
Le Chersonnex tiendra & Marceloyne,
La Thessalie vastera l'Amphipolle,
Mal incogneu & le refus d'Anthoine.

The awful plague at Perinthus and Nicopolis will take hold in the Peninsula and Macedonia. Thessaly and Amphibolis will be laid waste, an unknown evil refused by Anthony.

Logically we should end this examination of Nostradamus' great predictive work as we began. We started with the first prophecy of Century 1, so it is worth taking a look briefly at the one hundredth *quatrain* series. *Q100 (CX)* offers a strongly positive note for England,

period of time, although whether this is England or perhaps a wider European community is open to conjecture. He envisages troop movements on a large scale, and perhaps the chagrin of some old and spent colonial power is reflected in the reference to Portugal.

Interestingly, *Q100 (CIX)* also describes a victorious conclusion:

> *Navalle pugne nuit sera superée,*
> *Le feu aux naves à l'Occident ruiné*
> *Rubriche neufue la grande nef colorée,*
> *Ire à vainçu, & victoire en bruine.*

> *A naval battle will be won at night. Fire in the damaged western fleet. A new heading colours the {strategy} of the great ship. Anger to the vanquished and victory in the drizzle.*

Undoubtedly the most important of the 100 series *quatrains* for us, the readers, is that contained in Century VI. *Q100 (CVI)* is the only *quatrain* in the entire series to be penned in medieval Latin, and this in itself must bear major significance.

> *Quos legent hosce versus mature censunto*
> *Profanum vulgus & inscium ne attrectato*
> *Omnesq: Astrologi Blenni, Barbari procul sunto*
> *Qui aliter facit, is rite, sacer esto.*

> *May those who read this verse consider it with maturity. Let it not attract the profane and ignorant. May all astrologers, fools and barbarians keep their distance. He who does otherwise is the priest of the rite.*

The prophecy is provided, again unusually, with a heading:

LEGIS CANTIO CONTRA INEPTOS CRITICOS.

Incantation of the law against inept critics.

It speaks for itself.

although we are by now so far into the future that, whatever the prospect in store for these islands, the matter becomes academic.

> *Le grand empire sera par Angleterre*
> *Le pempotam des ans plus de trois cens:*
> *Grandes copies passer par mer & terre,*
> *Les Lusitains n'en seront pas contens.*

> *The great empire will be for England all powerful for more than 300 years. Powerful forces pass by land and sea. The Portuguese will not be content.*

Clearly this is Nostradamus in his allegorical mode. He sees one particular nation taking a hegemony for a long

WHAT CAN WE CONCLUDE FROM ALL OF THIS ANALYSIS *of obtuse four-line riddles couched in antiquated and adulterated language? Are there any real messages to be gained from the mass of predictive material which Michel de Notredame laboured over so earnestly in the final years of his life?*

RIDDLES
or VISIONS?

Was it a morbid game that he played to while away the remainder of a life which he had spent largely amongst victims of one of the most terrible natural afflictions ever to descend upon the human species? To what extent did the religious fanaticism and intolerance of his day play a part in his psychology and how much of his work was a reflection of the superstitions which influenced his generation of thinkers? What effect did it have on his outlook to be born into a European world of almost chronic strife and bloodshed?

Nostradamus warns us that his *Centuries* are not for idiots, nor for the profane, so we must set out to address his work intelligently and seriously, sympathetic to the man, his times and his aspirations.

One is tempted to conclude that Nostradamus was guilty of 'reverse engineering' whereby a device existed, that of prophecy, and he then worked out a stratagem of using it to maximum effect. If this was the case then he was inordinately shrewd in his course of action, proven by the enduring success and fascination of his work, yet to

AN EARLY-NINETEENTH-CENTURY ILLUSTRATION SHOWS NOSTRADAMUS AS ASTRONOMER AND SEER, AND AT HIS FEET THE WORK THAT WAS TO INTRIGUE THE WORLD FOR CENTURIES TO COME.

draw the conclusion is also cynical. There is no indication that Michel de Notredame was other than a modest and conscientious man who devoted much of his life to assisting others in grievous need so it is improbable that he would have left his epitaph in the form of a 'raspberry' of black comedy.

It is constantly pointed out, by past and present observers alike, that he was preoccupied with doom and gloom and that he predicted more or less constant strife for the human race during the entire span of his prophecies, however long in time that span may be. This, however, is a reflection of his times. In one way or another Europe was in an almost constant state of war during the sixteenth century and Nostradamus must have had scant optimism that this situation would ever change. What is equally revealing is that he seems to have anticipated, correctly, the amelioration of the medieval incidence of the plague and that it would then make only occasional revisitations upon humanity.

Concerning the apocalypse, the Second Coming, Nostradamus makes frequent allusions in line with the thinking of his day but he *never predicts* its actual arrival. In whichever way one examines his prophecies, either as a mad jumble of dating or in a chronological progression, they have no ending. The *Centuries* begin distinctly, demonstrated by the opening 'preface' in the first *quatrain* of Century I which finds him working alone in his study through the dark hours of the night. His works, however, seem not to be concluded in any finite manner. Perhaps this is because he never finished the task he had set himself so late in life. Century VII is only half completed, Centuries XI and XII are in much more of an embryonic state and have not constituted part of this analysis. It may be that, had the man lived for long enough, we should have seen a clear ending as well as a beginning.

As far as the bigoted religious climate of his day was concerned, Nostradamus seems to have avoided taking any overt swipes at the Catholic establishment. He occasionally predicts the ebb and flow of Christianity in the face of Islam and the rise and fall of pontiffs but little more, and he appears to have been more interested, generally, in the strategic and military changes in the world, coupled with some momentous events of a less martial nature. He foresaw the arrival of comets, eclipses and other celestial signs, and implicated them as harbingers of .earthquakes, droughts, famines and an assortment of dire events. But then was he not following the principle that every shrewd journalist follows: that good news is no news? 'Sunshine and roses' would not have attracted a vicariously morbid public to pore over his predictions in anything like the same magnitude as did details of future death and mayhem!

It is evident, from everything which he communicated to César, that Nostradamus feared that he would be branded a heretic or wizard with terrible consequences for himself and his family. He must have gained limited comfort from the fact that Catherine de Medici not only patronized him but also seems to have accepted his dire predictions about her family with resignation rather than irritation. Clearly she had implicit faith in his prophetic abilities and this conviction overrode any reservation about occultism and heresy since Catherine's displeasure could, very easily, have earned him a place before the Inquisition and a rendezvous with the stake. Nonetheless Nostradamus knew, realistically, that he was not immune from prosecution so he was prepared to render his

THE WAR IN HEAVEN DESCRIBED IN THE BOOK OF REVELATION, INTERPRETED HERE BY ALBRECHT DURER: THE APOCALYPSE WAS FREQUENTLY IN NOSTRADAMUS' THOUGHTS, THOUGH HE NEVER PREDICTED ITS ACTUAL ARRIVAL.

prophecies in ways which would not provide indictable evidence against him.

It is the manner in which he contrived to insure himself that has provoked the greatest controversy, yet the popular argument which suggests, figuratively, that he placed some 965 little pieces of paper in a hat, shook them up, and then collated them in the arbitrary sequence in which they emerged, is a silly one. It would have rendered the entire exercise meaningless and we can probably rest in reasonable certainty that his son César did not have

names of people linked with events and he then applied the tried and tested exercise of writing the predictions in antiquated and vague language which could often be interpreted in more than one way. This would have allowed him the defence against his accusers of saying: 'But that is your imaginative interpretation, I never wrote as much. Prove that I was referring to such-and-such!'

Secondly he introduced various 'red herrings' of chronology by incorporating, here and there, some prominent dates – probably too prominently placed to be anything other than pointers along false trails. He inserted just one accurate date, that of **Q72** **(CX)**, in order to provide a convenient starting point rather like the single completed answer from which to solve an enigma puzzle. The year 1999, near enough to 2000, is a simple one upon which to calculate his timescale.

It is not until one adopts the expedient of preparing a table and aligning the Centuries side by side, that patterns begin to emerge and we should ignore these patterns at our peril. The 64 and 66 series *quatrains*, to name a specific example out of many, offer too many similar references to be ignored. In the 64 series we find a false peace involving deceit detailed in Century VI, whilst the authorities in Geneva despair and become frustrated in Century II. In the 66 series we discover the overthrow of a great leader described in Century IV and the flight of a great leader outlined in Century II. We have drawn the conclusion that these clusters of seemingly corroborative predictions focus on the strategic situations in the eastern world including the conflict in Korea and the Chinese overthrow of Tibet in the 1950s.

In the *quatrain* 77 series there is too great a coincidence to be readily overlooked in the reference to the year seventeen *twenty-seven* in Century III and the number of years, *twenty-seven*, in Century VIII. The similarities in the 84 and 86 series are, again, glaringly obvious.

When all is said and done, there is no proof positive about Nostradamus' remarkable predictions, nor will there be unless, at some time in the future, new revelations emerge. Perhaps somewhere, mouldering between the pages of a time-worn, forgotten book on a dusty library shelf, there rests the authentic manuscript that will make everything clear. But we may be destined never to find

AN ARTIST'S IMPRESSION OF THE PRIMEVAL EARTH BEING BOMBARDED BY METEORITES. IT IS LITTLE WONDER THAT EXTRATERRESTRIAL ACTIVITY WAS REGARDED IN THE MIDDLE AGES AS A HARBINGER OF DOOM.

some complicated code-breaking device to hand that would enable him to sort out the jumble. If he had such a key we would surely know about it.

Nostradamus' interest lay in protecting his prophecies only against the peculiar logic that he anticipated would be employed by the Church and its Commission of Inquiry. In order to achieve this aim he used two simple devices. He avoided, to a large extent, the incorporation of concrete answers and in many ways it would be a shame to do so. If such a revelation were to come to light it would take away the magic, destroy that which our imagination holds dear and bring the enduring romance of Michel de Notredame firmly to earth.

More than this, however, it would open the serious question of whether humankind is, after all, in control of its own destiny or whether there is some greater power which has our future mapped out for us in minute detail. Should we understand, or even begin to believe that this were true, the world might rapidly descend into chaos. One of the great guiding principles of civilized society lies in the conviction that we are responsible for our own actions and, assuming that we adopt any kind of faith in a spiritual dimension to our lives, that we will be judged on some altered plane according to how we have handled that mortal responsibility. Should we come to a recognition that our earthly actions are individually and collectively determined from outside, and are pre-programmed into our subconscious, the sense of responsibility whereby we conduct ourselves in a moral fashion will rapidly diminish.

There is also a question of what conflicts went through Nostradamus' mind. Here was a man brought up in a society plagued not only by disease but by religious fervour and superstition. Both his cultural Jewish roots and the climate of Roman Catholicism in which he was raised promoted, in their differing styles, the same ideology. They subscribed to the view of a world in which human fallibility and sin were largely voluntary, brought about by mortal weakness, and only the celestial punishment was inevitable. To propose proof that this power of self-regulation was all a nonsense would not just have offended the ecclesiastical establishment, it must also have given Nostradamus cause for considerable introspection.

One conclusion is beyond doubt, evidenced by the sheer weight of inventive solutions to Nostradamus' riddles that have been conjectured down the four hundred and fifty or so years since his death. The infinite variety of meanings, most of which stand up to disconcertingly convincing inspection, indicates that whatever style of coat we have a mind to fashion from his *quatrains*, Nostradamus always manages to provide just the right cloth from which to cut it. If we seek evidence of

Napoleon's victories and defeats he hands it to us. If we wish to cite the same material as evidence of his anticipation of the Second World War, it somehow moulds itself conveniently to our requirement.

In this respect, if in no other, Nostradamus was probably the greatest prophetic genius of all time. As for the rest, it was for him to know and for us, endlessly, to ponder! Michel de Notredame died on the night of 1st July 1566 at the age of sixty-two. He had, not surprisingly, already predicted the exact manner of his death.

A LIGHTNING BOLT BRIEFLY ILLUMINATES A NIGHT-TIME ROOFSCAPE. THOUGH THE CAUSE OF THESE ELECTRICAL CHARGES IS NOW WELL UNDERSTOOD BY SCIENCE, THEY REMAIN A POWERFUL SYMBOL OF CELESTIAL WRATH AND CONTINUE TO MESMERIZE US EVEN TODAY.

INDEX

ACKNOWLEDGEMENTS

The publishers would like to thank the following sources for their kind permission to reproduce the pictures in this book:

Lorna Ainger: 112

Bridgeman Art Library, London: British Library, London, Signs of the Zodiac *Planisphaerium Copernicanum*, c.1543, devised by Copernicus (1473–1543) 24, Louvre, Paris, France/Giraudon, The Goddess Hathor placing the magic collar on Seti I, taken from the tomb of Seti I in the Valley of the Kings, New Kingdom, 19th Dynasty (1314-1200BC) (painted limesstone relief) 26, Museo e Gallerie Nazionali di Capodimonte, Naples/Giraudon, Marble bust of Julius Caesar 33t,Tretyakov Gallery, Moscow, The Last Judgement, icon from the Novgorod school, 15th century by Novgorod School (15th century) 36

Jean Loup Charmet: 7, 19, 21t, 29, 44, 45, 50, 51b, 61, 62, 66, 94, 122

Corbis: Roger Antrobus 65, Bettmann 64, 70-78, 79t, 81, 82, 85/Reuters 86, 108/UPI 37, 87, Jonathan Blair 106, Bojan Brecelj 114, Howard Davies 100t, Bernard and Catherine Desjeux 102, Peter Russell/The Military Picture Library 120, Peter Turnley 100b, Penny Tweedie 110, US Dept. of Energy-Nevada 38/9; USGS-Hawaii Volcano Observatory 41, Adam Woolfit 107

Et archive: 3, 15, 23b, 35, 52, 63, 109t/Bibliotheque Nationale, Paris 20, 48, Musee Carnavalet, Paris 10, Museo Correr Venice 105, National Maritime Museum 54, Prado Madrid 109b, Private Collection 43

Mary Evans Picture Library: 1, 22, 23t, 28, 42, 46, 49, 53, 55, 57, 59, 60, 113, 115, 123/Explorer 12, 31, Explorer/ADPC 51t; Fawcett Library 18

Robert Harding Picture Library: Bildagentur Schuster/Krauskopf 104

Image Select: 5, 16, 103/Ann Ronan 8, 11, 14, 21b, 27, 33b, 58, 117

Popperfoto: Reuters 91

Science Photo Library: 68, 79b/Julian Baum 98, Tony Craddock 110t, Eric Grave 111t, David A Hardy 124, Keith Kent 4, R.Maisonneuve, Publiphoto Diffusion 111b, Peter Menzel 99, NASA, Institute for Space Studies 101, NIBSC 119, NOAA 116, Dr Morley Read 118, Rouxaime & Jacana 125, Frank Zullo 96-7

Topham Picturepoint: 80, 83, 84, 93/Associated Press 90, 92, J. Bauluz 88, A.Emric 89

Every effort has been made to acknowledge correctly and contact the source and/copyright holder of each picture, and Carlton Books Limited apologises for any unintentional errors or omissions which will be corrected in future editions of this book.